DICTIONARY OF PHILOSOPHY

DICTIONARY OF PHILOSOPHY

Edited by
S. C. SINHA

ANMOL PUBLICATIONS PVT. LTD.
NEW DELHI-110 002 (INDIA)

ANMOL PUBLICATIONS PVT. LTD.
Regd. Office: 4360/4, Ansari Road, Daryaganj,
New Delhi-110002 (India)
Tel.: 23278000, 23261597, 23286875, 23255577
Fax: 91-11-23280289
Email: anmolpub@gmail.com
Visit us at: www.anmolpublications.com

Branch Office: No. 1015, Ist Main Road, BSK IIIrd Stage
IIIrd Phase, IIIrd Block, Bengaluru-560 085 (India)
Tel.: 080-41723429 • Fax: 080-26723604
Email: anmolpublicationsbangalore@gmail.com

Dictionary of Philosophy

First Edition, 1991

Reprint, 1998, 2001, 2007, 2012

PRINTED IN INDIA

Printed at Himanshu Printers, Delhi.

Preface

This dictionary provides instant access to relevant terminology in every facet of philosophy from A to Z. Some terms have been explained briefly, others at length.

Every effort has been carefully made to write the entries in a clear and lucid style to provide both straight forward definitions and invaluable background information.

This dictionary will be of immense value to undergraduate and post-graduate students, college teachers, university teachers and school administrators.

When a dictionary of this kind is being compiled, it becomes essential to draw upon the work of many authorities and seeks the advice of colleagues to all of whom the editor is deeply indebted.

Finally, the editor expresses his sincere thanks to the publisher and printer for printing this book promptly.

All comments from users on omissions or shortcomings will be most welcome.

THE EDITOR

A

Abandonment. The term used for one of the central ideas of atheistic existentialists, like Sartre. As God does not exist there can be no objective values or meaning to life; thus man is thrust out into the world, "abandoned". He must make decisions, distinguish right from wrong, but as there is no guiding hand he is thrown back entirely on himself.

Abduction

From the Latin ab ("away") and ducere ("to lead").

(1) In Aristotle abduction refers to those types of syllogistic inference which fail to carry certainty with them, whether due to a weak connection between the major and middle terms, or the middle and minor terms

(2) For C.S. Peirce (8), abduction is one of three basic forms of inference, along with induction and deduction. Abduction is the means whereby hypotheses are generated, moving from a particular case to a possible explanation of the case.

Abhinivesha. Sanskrit term signifying the love of life and fear of death. One of the five kinds of delusive attachment of the Yoga system.

Absolute. A term which was used by post-Kantian idealist metaphysicians to cover the totality of what really exists, a totality thought of as a unitary system somehow both generating all apparent diversity.

Absolute Space. Space considered as an entity within which bodies are placed, and which itself has real properties, such as shape or extension.

Absolute Suchness. Ashvaghosa's name for reality.

Absolutism. The opposite of 'relativism', and hence infected with all the same ambiguity and indeterminacy.

Abstract Ideas. If words are employed meaningfully then, surely, the user must have an idea of what they mean; indeed perhaps that idea is the meaning? Granted this seductively obvious assumption, then a question arises about such general words as 'man', or 'animal', or 'triangle'. Since they cannot refer to anything individual and particular, may be what is involved is abstract ideas conceived as special kinds of mental images.

Abstraction. From the Latin abstractus, past participle of the verb abstrahere ("to draw from").

(1) In Aristotelian and Scholastic philosophy abstraction refers to the process whereby universal ideas come to be appropriated by the mind. Abstraction is possible because of the hylomorphic nature of substance, *i.e.*, that substance is composed of matter and form. The mind receives a sense datum or phantasm and draws out the form, thus providing a universal for intellectual use

(2) For Locke abstraction takes place by drawing out what has been common to a group of individual things, on the basis of a comparison of their similarities and differences.

Absurdity. In the vulgar sense, obvious falsity or opposition to common sense or reason.

Accident. From the Latin accidens, present participle of accidere, "to happen".

In Aristotelian and Scholastic philosophy, that mode of being which inheres in some other being, such as the mode of existence of the redness in an apple. To be contrasted with substantial being, such as the mode of existence of the apple itself. Not only a quality such as redness, however, but any of the nine Aristotelian categories other than substance itself.

Academy of Athens. In effect, the first university, established by Plato about 385 BC.

Acceptance. One possible reaction to a theory or to evidence. A philosopher of science who believes that evidence never decisively proves or refutes a scientific theory may conclude that acceptance of a theory ought always to be provisional or partial.

Accident

1. (in scholastic philosophy) the term refers to that which in itself has no independent or self-sufficient existence, but only inheres in a substance.

2. (in Aristotelian logic). This term refers to inessential property, that which may be attributed to a substance without being essential to that substance. For instance, a girl may be blonde, but she must be female; blondeness in this example is an accident, femaleness is not.

Acosmism. From the Greek a ("not") and kosmos ("world"). The term was coined by Hegel to refer to the doctrine that the world is unreal and that only God exists Hegel applied the term to the philosophy of Spinoza, but that may be a mis-application. Term fits more exactly the Acosmic Pantheism of Shankara.

Acrasia (or **Akrasia**). (Greek for : weakness). An alternative name for weakness of the will. The term has been derived from the Aristotelian distinction between the akrates, the morally weak man, and the enkrates, the man who can resist temptation.

Act. A Latin term which has been derived from agere ("to do"). The Greek term is energeia.

(1) Aristotle contrasted act (energeia) with potency (dynamis), associating the former with form and the latter with matter.

(2) The same contrast in Scholastic philosophy is between actus and potentia. A distinction is made between first and second act. By "first act" is meant the form of a thing, and by "second act" the operation of the thing. "Act" suggests in this terminology both actuality and activity. In contrast to other beings, God is regarded as actus purus.

Action. A word which is sometimes applied to things (for example, the action of acid on metal), but primarily relating to the doings of purposive agents. Aristotle distinguished an action—what a man does (poiesis)—from what merely happens to him (pathos : usually translated affection' or 'passion').

Action at a Distance. The use of the term implies a remote and instantaneous influence by the body, without any apparent mechanism for transmitting the force produced.

Actuality and Potentiality. Actuality (Greek : energeia) refers to that mode of being in which a thing can bring other things about or be brought about by them—the realm of events and facts. By contrast, potentiality (Greek : dynamis) refers to not a mode in which a thing exists, but rather the power to effect change, the capacity of a thing to make transitions into different states.

Actus Purus. A Latin term which means "pure act" or "pure actuality." This is the appropriate name for God in Scholastic philosophy. As purely actual, God is the one being without potentiality ; hence the highest, or only complete.

Adam Kadmon. The term used for the hermaphroditic, primordial man of the Cabala.

AD HOC. The Latin phrase, meaning "to this," suggests the directional character of the ad hoc. In the logic of explanation an ad hoc hypothesis is one formed to explain a given phenomenon, but differing from powerful hypotheses in not being derivable from other phenomena or yielding other testable consequences.

An Hominem Argument] (Latin for : argument directed at a man.) The term is used for two kinds of argument. The first kind has been a fallacious argument (see fallacy) whereby the premises merely attack a particular man (for example, for his unwholesome moral character) while the conclusion purports to establish the falsity of a thesis he holds.

The second kind is an argument taking as its premise something that has been accepted by the other party but not perhaps by the arguer and deducing a consequence unacceptable to that other party.

Adoptionism. The theological doctrine that Christ, born as a mortal being, became the Son of God by adoption. The doctrine, appearing in several forms in the first three centuries A.D., led to the Adoptionist Controversy in 8th-century Spain, and was condemned in the Charlemagne-sponsored synods of 792,794, and 799.

Ad Quem. From the Latin ad ("to") and quem ("which"). The phrase, along with ad quod ("to what") is used in referring to the end point, tendency, or goal of an argument or chain of reasoning. To be contrasted with a quo, referring to the corresponding beginning point.

Advaita. Sanskrit term which means "nonquality." The term refers to the central idea of the Vedantic philosophy that man's self (the atman), and the soul of all things (the Brahman) are identical. The school of Indian thought stressing nonquality is known as Advaita Vedanta. The religio-philosophical task of human life is no dispel our mistaken beliefs in quality, including, of course, the belief in our separateness from Brahman. The chief representatives of the school are Gaudapada and Shankara.

Adventitious Ideas. Refers to one of Descartes, three classes of ideas, along with "factitious" and "innate". Adventitious ideas come from experience, entering the mind through sensation.

Aeon Among Valentinian Gnostics, especially, the name given to the semi-divine, spiritual intermediaries emanating from God and the material world, which meant—in their view—bridging between good and evil.

Aesthetics. From the Greek aisthesis ("sensation"). This term has come to designate not the whole domain of the sensible, but only that portion to which the term "beauty" may apply.

Affect. A term used in the rational psychology of Spinoza to name the variety of feelings, purposes, and drives which motivate us. As the affects are internal their influence upon us would seem to allow a kind of self-determination.

A Fortiori. A Latin phrase which means "all the more" or "with the greater force." A type of argument in which two cases are compared, a lesser and a greater. The argument runs from the lesser to the greater case. If from the lesser case one is able to gain a certain consequence how much more certain one should be able to except this consequence, or a stronger result, in the greater case.

After Image. Refers to the visual version of what psychologists called 'after-sensation', wherein a visual image resembling an observed object persists after the external stimulus assumed to have caused it has been withdrawn.

Agape. Greek term which means "selfless love." The term is derived from tne Agape or "love feast" of the early Christians, a common meal to promote "Christian fellowship" frequently associated with the sacrament.

Agni. A Sanskrit term which means "fire." One of the most important of the Vedic gods, Agni was god of the alter fire ; and also represented the trinity of earthly fire, lightning and sun. In this extended sense he was the mediator between the gods and man.

Agnosticism. From the Greek a ("not") and gignoskein ("to know"). A term coined by T H. Huxlay to express a position of suspended belief. Huxley used the term to apply to any proposition for which the evidence was insufficient for belief. It is usually, however, applied principally to suspension to belief with respect to God.

Ahimsa. (Sanskrit for : non-injury.) The doctrine, particularly supported by the Jains and Buddhists, that it is wrong to kill another living thing, however humble. The belief underlying this doctrine is that all living creatures possess souls of essentially the same kind, and because of transmigration) (metempsychosis) the soul of some revered ancestor may be temporarily inhabiting some lowly animal form.

Ai. From the Chinese, meaning "love." For Mo Tzu (q v.3) and Han Yu, key term in achieving the good and right.

Ajativada. Sanskrit which means "No-Origination." A doctrine of Gaudapada holding the sole reality to be the Absolute.

Aksara. From Sanskrit, meaning "imperishable." Used in the Upanishads as an alternative name for Brahman.

Alchemy. A medieval philosophy which combines an occult cosmology with practical chemical experimentation.

Alexandrian School. The term used for a centre of Neoplatonism in 5th and 6th.century Alexandria. Unlike its rival at Athens the Alexandrian School became Christian, concentrating on scholarly commentary, rather than theurgy and metaphysical speculation. It survived the capture of Alexandria by the Arabs (641 AD) and transmitted much Neoplatonist learning to the Middle Ages.

Algebra of Logic. The name applied in the 19th century to that development, influenced by mathematics, beyond traditional logic. Contributing significantly to this developmen were Boole, De Morgan· Jevons, Peirce, Venn, and Schroder, each of which.

Algorithm. Derived from Al-Khwarizmi of Al-Korisimi, the surname of the author of a famous 9th-century Arabic work on arithmetic which was translated into Latin. All such books were called Algorismus, and so the term came to mean the operations of arithemetic in Arabic notation. It how refers to any sort of logical or mathematical operation with any sort of notation.

Alienans. A medieval term which distinguishes certain adjectives that form peculiarly tight relations with the nouns to which they are applied.

Alienation

(1) Marx's view of alienation is described in his Economic and Philosophical Manuscripts of 1844 (q.v. Max 1). It is a process of the concretization of man's inner nature which then becomes property, and separates one man from another.

(2) In a more general sense the alienated individual is a theme often treated in Existentialism perhaps most clearly in the concept of inauthenticity.

ALS OB. From German, which means "as if." A key term of the way men learn to control experience through the construction of fictional entites.

Alteration. For Aristotle one of three basic types of change, namely "change of quality," to be distinguished from growth and diminution which is "change of quantity," and locomotion, which is "change of place."

Altruism. From Latin alter which is means "other". Coined by the French philosopher, Auguste Comte. The term implies regard for and devotion to the interests of others, even to the sacrifice of persnol interest.

Altruism and Egoism. As a philosophical term 'altrusmi' may most usefully be seen in opposition to (ethical) 'egosim'. Egosim rests on the hypothesis that morality can be explained ultimately in term of self- interest, albeit so called enlightened self-interest. For the egoist, the apparent conflicts between the demands of morality and of persnol gain are merely conflicts between different aspect of our self-interest—indirect v. direct or longterm v. short-term.

Ambiguity. A word, term, or expression is to be ambiguous, or to have the property, "ambiguity," when it is capable of having more than a single sense. Ambiguity can lead to the fallacy of Equivocation.

Amitabha. The term used for the Savior of the Pure Land sect of Mahayana Buddhism also the reincarnated Pantshen Lama of Lamaism.

Ampliative. From Latin ampliare which means "to make wider.

"Ampliative judgment" and "synthetic judgment" have been identical in meaning, referring to judgment whose predicates have been not implicit in the meanings of their subject terms. "Synthetic judgment" contrasts with "analytic judgement" as ampliative judgement" contrasts with explicative judgement".

"Ampliative inference" on the other hand refers to the type of inference in which something predicated in the conclusion is not found in the premises, *i.e.*, that form of induction in which by analogy one affirms one affairs of the whole what was found to be true of a part of the whole.

Anagogical Interpretation. From the Greek and ("up") and agoge ("a leading"). The term is used to refer to interpretations, usually of Scripture, leading one "upward," *i.e.*, toward the spiritual or mystical. The anagogical has been thus a type of allegorical interpretation.

Analogia Entis. A Latin term which means "analogy of being.

Analogies of Experience. For Kant the a priori principles making possible the unity of human experience. The three principles deriving from the category of Relation, have been substance, causality, and reciprocity. For Kant the principles have been derived from the basic types of propositions, and imply the orderings of substance, cause, and community according to which we interpret experience.

Analogy. From Greek ana ("according to") and logos ("ratio, proportion"). This term refers to the relation of similarity between two or more things allowing the drawing of probable or necessary conclusions depending on the kind of relation in question.

Analysis, Intentional. A type of analysis which was introduced by Husserl taking the intentional aspect of experience to be fundamental, and exhibiting the development of all philosophy from this starting point.

Analysis, Philosophical. According to Ayer refers to analysis function of philosophy, and consists of translating sentences needing clarification into other sentences which contain neither the key words of the original sentences, nor synonyms for them.

Analytic. From Greek analytikos, derived from the verb analyein, "to resolve into its elements.

(1) Aristotle used the term to name his logical treatises : the Prior Analytics containing his analysis of the syllogism, the Posterior Analytics containing analyses of the conditions of demonstrable knowledge.

(2) Kant in the section of his first critique, called "Transcendental Analytic," analysed the functions of reason within experience, especially with respect to its contribution to the structured phenomena of our experience. The main burden of the Transcendental Analytic concerned with the deduction of the categories present in experience.

Analytic Judgement, Statement, or Proposition. A judgement, statement, or proposition having the properties of necessity and universality by virtue of the fact that the predicate of the judgment is a result of analysis of the subject term.

Analyticity. Refers to the study of the nature of, and conditions necessary for, analytic judgments.

Anamnesis. A Greek term meaning "to recall to memory." Plato's doctrine of knowledge as recollection of the ideas known to the soul in a previous existence, and forgotten in the trauma of birth.

Ananda. See sat chist Ananda.

Anarchism. This term is used to designate a variety of doctrines centering on the belief that the organized state is the cause of injustice among men and should be eliminated. The means of its elimination varies with the anarchists ; the points of view include evolutionsists and revolutionists, those committed to violence and those committed to non-violence.

Anastikaya. Sanskrit term which means "nonphysical." Used in Jainism in the phrase anastikaya dravya ("nonphysical substance").

Anaximenes of Miletus. A younger compatriot of Anaximander of Miletus. He held that air is the fundamental matter, which takes on other forms and appearances by condensation and rarefaction. These derivative substances, he may have thought, became in their turn the elements of compounds. His other cosmological notions, being closer to popular traditions, are less interesting, but there was some meteorological speculation, using the conception of rarefying and condensing air.

Angst. German term which means "dread." A basic fact of human nature, according to existentialist philosophy, Angst is a nameless fear which has no object.

Anima. (Latin for : soul).

1. See soul.

2. (in Jungian psychology) The part of the collective unconscious within an individual that represents the feminine aspect of man's nature.

Animal Soul. Refers to an analogue in animals of the human soul or mind. In opposition to the Cartesian view that man alone possessed a soul, the doctrine of animal soul claimed that animal behaviour was not physicalistically explicable, but implied mental functioning and the existence of soul.

Animism. Refers to the view that everything in the Universe, including even plants and inanimate objects, has some kind of psychological being more or less tenously similar to that of human and non-human animals. Thus it has been asserted that a stone has been not only an aggregate of moving molescules but has 'awareness' of other bodies in, for example, attracting and repelling them or being affected along with them gravity. When this theory is held by primitive peoples, it is called animism. Philosophical animists have often been described, more politely, as 'panphschists' Doctrines of this sort have been held by numerous thinkers, including Empedocles, Plotinus, Leibniz, Schopenhaur, Peirce, Schiller, Whitehead, Alexander, de Chardin, and Waddington.

An Sich

(1) In the Kantian philosophy a thing or event independent of experience.

(2) In Hegal the term is also used, but there the an sich is not only separate from consciousness but therefore in large measure potential, latent, undeveloped or impoverished.

(3) The term is also used by Sartre the French phrase being en soi. Sartre distinguishes between the en soi, or "in itself," and the pour soi, or "for itself." The former is applied to that which is without, and the latter to that which possesses, awareness.

Antecedent. In sentences, or propositions, of the form "if A, then B" A is called the antecedent, and B the consequent (q.v. Proposition 2).

Anthropocentrism. From the Greek anthropos ("man") and kentron ("center"). The view that man is, or must look upon himself as, the center of reality. This not a philosophical concept in itself but the term has analogies to the view of Protagoras that "man is the measure of all things."

Anthropology, Philosophical. The term, literally means "philosophical knowledge of man." It applies to those studies which treat man as a "whole being," attempting to avoid or go beyond approaches in which man is regarded merely as a scientific object.

Anthropomorphism. From the Geek anthropomorphos ("of human form"). This term refers to the attribution of human qualities to the divine; thus, the conceiving of God or the gods in human form.

Anthropopathism. From the Greek anthropos ("man") and pathein ("suffering"). A term which was coined by the writer and critic John Ruskin (1819 1900) to designate the state of mind leading to what he called the "pathetic fallacy," *i.e.*, emotional strain or grief leading the poet to ascribe to nature the emotions of sympathy or cruelty.

Anthroposophy. Q.v. Steiner.

Anthroposophy. Refers to an occult system which claims that the key to wisdom and to an understanding of the Universe lies in man himself.

Antichrist. This term simply means one who denies Christ. In extension, however, the term signifies a great force, filling the world with evil, whose defeat will lead to the Second Coming. In the extended sense the Antichrist has been taken to be, at different times, the Roman Empire, specific emperors (*e.g.*, Nero), Mohammed, and the popes themselves.

Anticipations of Experience. Kant's doctrine that all sensations are having some intensive magnitude or degree. According to Kant we can know this in advance of experience, although we cannot know in advance what the quality or degree would be.

Antilogism. From the Greek antilogismos which means "a counter-charge." The term refers to a method of checking on the validity of a syllogism.

Antinomianism. From the Greek anti ("against") and nomos ("law"). The name of a recurred tendency in Christian history to reject the law—Mosaic, ecclesiastical, or every moral—as no longer binding, and to substitute faith alone. The problem of the relation of the Mosaic law to the Gospel is treated in the writings of the Apostle Paul (q.v.). Among the groups with antinomian tendencies one might mention the Gnostics (q.v), the Marcionites (q.v. Marcion), and the Manichoeans (q.v.). A recrudescene of the tendency occurred in the 16th and 17th centuries with Familists, Davidists, and Adamists. Luther (q v.) and Melanchthon (q v.) were involved in one such controversy, settled by the Formula of Concord.

Antinomianism. Refers to the view that ordinary moral laws are not applicable to Christians, whose lives, it is said, are governed solely by divine grace. Opponents of this position have always pointed, during its not infrequent recurrences, to its alarming ethical implications.

Antinomy. Refers to an obsolescent synonym for paradox or contradiction.

Antithesis. From the Greek anti ("against") and tithenai ("to set"). Etymologically, the term has been comparable in meaning to "antinomy" and "contradiction."

(1) In Kant's "Antinomies of Pure Reason" the "antithesis" is the negative member of the antinomy, the one opposing thesis.

(2) In Fichte and in Hegel "antithesis" is the middle member of the triad, opposing the thesis ; the opposition of thesis and antithesis is resolved by the synthesis, the third member of the triad.

Antonym. A word of contrary meaning : 'good' is an antonym of 'bad'.

Apodeictic. (or apodictic). A term which is used in Aristotelian logic to indicate the mode or modality of a proposition. An apodeictic proposition refers to one that asserts that something is necessarily the case or that something is possible, as for example 'Seven cannot be more than nine'.

Apagoge. From the Greek opo ("from") and agein ("to lead").

(1) In Aristotelian logic an abductive syllogism.

(2) The method of indirect demonstration whereby one demonstrates the absuridity of the conclusion contradictory to one which to be established.

Apathia A Latin term from the Greek apatheia, which is derived from a ("not") and pathos ("suffering"). This Greek virtue of utter tranquility served as the most important value for the Stoic. It has to be compared to the state of ataraxia stressed among the Epicureans.

Apeiron. A Greek term which means "boundless, indeterminate, infinite."

(1) In Anaximander that from which all determinate being comes, and into which it goes.

(2) For the Phythagoreans one of two principles : Unlimited (apeiron) which opposes the limit (peras).

Apocalypse. From the Greek apokaluptein ("to uncover or disclose"). The doctrine that the world is soon to be destroyed by fire, purified from evil, and that the righteous would be resurrected to live in a purified order of things. Popular in the last centuries before Christ, the doctrine generated a body of apocalyptical literature. Daniel, Revelation, and a number of the books of the Apocrypha belong to this literature.

Apocatastasis. Fron the Greek apokatastasis which means "complete restoration." A concept of universal salvation hely by Origen the theologian.

Apodictic or Apodeictic. From the Greek apo ("from") and deiknynai ("to show"). In logic and metaphysics the term applies to propositions or judgements. Apodictic propositions and judgments are necessary, that is without alternative.

Apodosis. A Greek term which means "a giving back," the term refers to the "then" clause of an if then statement. The conditional clause has been the protasis.

Apollinarianism. The Christological doctrine that in Jesus the Logos (a perfect divine nature) assumed a human body, exercising the functions ordinarily performed by the human mind.

Apology. Refers to a form of discourse in defense of one's position. Among the most famous instances of such discourse one may cite Plato's Apology, giving Socrates' defense of his philosophic life and mission the entire movement of early Christian apologists and Cardinal Newman's Apologia pro Vita Sua, where he defends his philosophical and religious development, including his leaving the Anglican Church for Catholicism.

Apophantic Judgment. From the Greek apohansis ("proposition"). The subject-predicate form of judgment throught by Aristotle to be basic.

Aporetic. Raising questions and objections, without necessarily providing answers. Such a procedure is characteristic of Socrates in the early dialogues of Plato. A difficulty of this sort is sometimes labelled, by Ryle and others, and aporia (Greek for : puzzle).

Apostasy. From the Greek apostasia ("a defection"). In Roman Catholicism a total desertion of, or departure from, one's faith or from holy orders or from the monastic state. A formal apostate has been subject to excommunication.

A Posteriori. From the Latin a ("form") and posteriori ("the later"). The term is used to designate a kind of knowledge which can be gained only from experience ; hence, it can be formulated only after observation or experiment.

Apotheosis. From the Greek apo ("from") and theoun ("to deify"). The elevation of a mortal to the rank of a god. Virtually all cultures show evidence of the transformation of heroes and rules into divinities.

Apperance. In the history of philosophy the term stands in constrast to reality. At times the relation is that of illusion or falsity to turth. Most often, however, at least in Western philosophy, the relation is that of opinion—that which may or not be ture—to truth.

Apperception. Self-consciousness or inner awareness, in contrast with 'perception', denoting outer awareness.

Appetites. From the Latin oppetere ("to strive after, long for"). The term applies to the dynamic, striving aspect of human nature.

Appetition. The term is sometimes used to apply to the process of satisfying the appetites.

Appropriation. Refers to the subjective approach to truth favored by Kierkegaard. He contrasted his view with objective approach of science, which he called "endless approximation," and which and which he opposed.

A Priori From the Latin a ("from") and priori ("the preceding"). Used in contrast to a posteriori to refer to those conclusions which we derive from what has already been laid down, and not from experience. Thus, it refers to what we can derive from our definitions and what is implicit in the meanings of ideas already accepted.

Apriorism. Refers to the philosophical position, opposed to empiricism, held by those who characteristically consider that the mind is furnished with innate ideas and that there exists the possibility of genuine knowledge independent of experience.

Aquinas, St. Thomas (1225-1274). Medieval philosopher theologian.

A QUO. From the Latin a ("from") and quo ("which"). The phrase, part of the vocabulary of Scholastic philosophy, refers to the point of origin of an argument, that is, to the principles, assumptions, and definitions from which it is derived.

Arbor Porphyii. The Tree of Porphyri, a manner of illustrating the relations of genus, species, and individuals, widely influential throughout the Middle Ages.

Arche. A Greek term with significy "that which was in the beginning."

Archelaus of Athens. A pupil of Anaxagoras and teacher of Socrates. His small contribution, to cosmology rather than philosophy, seems to have consisted in amending the system of Anaxagoras, using elements drawn from other predecessors.

Archetype. From the Greek arche ("primal") plus typos ("figure" or "pattern"). For Plato the original forms or ideas in which things participate and of which they are copies. In Scholasticism the archetypes have as their location the divine mind. In Locke the term shifts in meaning to signify things in the world, the originals of our ideas. With Jung another shift occurs, and the term refers to the primordial of the collective unconscious.

Architectonic. The term used to describe a philosophical system constructed according to a consistent plan.

Arete. The Greek term for virtue. It is a fulfillment term. For Aristotle who may be taken to represent the Greeks in this respect, arete is the fulfillment of the function of being human.

Argument. See function q v. Peirce (16).

Argumentum Ad Judicicum. An argument relying on the judicious sense or common sense of mankind.

Argument from (or to) Design. By far the most popular and widely persuasive of all the tradional arguments for the existence of/

God, also called the teleological argument. It is usual to proceed not from admitted instances of design deductively but from observations of regularity and integration, by some sort of argument from experience, to the conclusion that these must be the work of a Designer. It is therefore better, and now becoming more usual, to say not argument from but argument to design.

Argumentum Ad Baculum. An argument employing an implicit or explicit threat.

Argumentum Ad Rem. An argument which adheres to the point, hence avoiding the fallacies which involve moving away from the point at issue in one of a great variety of ways.

Argumentum Ex Concesso. An argument which takes as its basis the propositions conceded to be true by one's opponent.

Arianism. 4th cent. A.D. The name of a dispute which wracked the early church, continued from 318 to 381 A.D. The subject of the dispute was the meaning of the incarnation in relation to the Christian premise of monotheism.

Aristocracy. From the Greek aristos ("best"; and kratein ("to rule") One of the perennially formulated types of ideal government, aristocracy implies rule by the best in the interests of the whole society but without the participation of the governed.

(1) For Plato aristocracy was the ideal social structure, standing in contrast to four degenerate forms of goverment.

(2) For Aristotle on the other hand, aristocracy was one of three desirable forms of government, sharing Aristotle's commendation with monarchy and polity.

Aristotle. 384-322 B.C. Greek philosopher. Born in Stagyra, Macedonia. Son of Nicomachus, physician to the king. At 18 entered Plato's Academy, and studied there nearly 20 years.

In Metaphysics Aristotle explicitly criticizes Plato's theory of Forms, alluding to the third man argument and complaining that the Forms are useless as explanatory devices and that the various arguments for accepting the Forms either prove nothing or establish the existence of unwelcome Forms such as negations and relations.

In the Categories, for example, individual things such as particular men and animals are called primary substances; species and genera (genus) of primary substances are called secondary substances. The species and genera are what an individual thing is; Socrates is a man (species) and an animal (genus).

Aristotle adds that it is characteristic of both primary and secondary realities (substances) not to have contraries. Many of Plato's Forms come in contrary pairs, for example, the large and the small.

In the Posterior Analytics, a treatise on the logical structure of a science, Aristotle argues for the autonomy of various disciplines (geometry, astronomy, harmony) and against there being principles common to all sciences, from which the correct explanations given in those sciences could be deduced. Acceptance of this would undermine the hopes that Plato, at one stage at least, held of dialectic Plato's Republic speaks of dialectic as pursuing the most general principles from which even the principles of mathematics can be derived.

Aristotle does conclude that the best (and happiest) man spends as much time as possible in the purest activity of reason, theorizing (Ethics X). However, since he is a man, the rational part of his soul (psyche) is more than just an intellect, and intellectual excellence by itself does not make a good and happy man. Reason governs action as well as theorizing. Action is the response made to desire, and here, Aristotle insists, one can respond too much or too little. The correct response lies somewhere between the two extremes This is the doctrine of the mean (golden mean). It does not pretend to provide a moral decision procedure. It is a (meta-ethical) statement about the form of certain moral coneepts : to every virtue there are two distinct vices.

Arithmetic, Foundations of

(1) Peano demonstrated that all of the natural numbers and their relations can be deduced from five postulates.

(2) Dedekind discovered how to define real numbers in terms of rational numbers.

(3) Frege demonstrated the possibility of defining rational numbers in terms of logical entities.

(4) Russell and Whitehead developed this program in their Principia Mathematica, thus basing arithmetic on logic.

Ars Combinatoria. A Latin phrase which means the "combinatory art." The phrase was used by Leibniz (q.v. 11-12) to signify the general program of building complex concepts from simple ones according to rule.

Art. From the Latin ars signifying any purposeful making or doing.

(1) In Plato art is the activity or object of any making or doing controlled by the movement down from theory to practice, and contrasting with the upward movement toward theory.

(2) In Aristotle art is one of three branches of knowledge.

(3) Aquinas follows both of his predecessors, defining art as right reason in making thing.

Artha-Sastra, The. See Kautilya.

Articles of Faith. Propositions concerning the interpretation of a religion which have to be taken on faith.

Asana. From the Sanskrit, which means "sitting." In Yoga and other systems of Indian philosophy, the emphasis on posture as one of the conditions of spiritual progress.

Asanga. 4th or 5th Century A D.

Indian philosopher. Founder of the Yogachara (Way of Yoga) or Consciousness-Only School. In the founding of the school he was assisted by his younger brother, Vasubandhu (q.v.) who was known as the systematizer of the position.

Principal writings: Mahayanabhidhar-masangiti-shastra; Mahayanasam-parigraha-shastra; Mahayanasutralankara-shastra.

(1) Like certain of his predecessors in Mahayana Buddhism he held that reality is devoid of plurality, and that all phenomena are subjective in character. His addition was to hold that the nature of the real is pure consciousness.

(2) Surrounded by illusion—even the empirical ego is part of this illusion—the way of liberation requires the destruction of this illusion. One will first realize the imaginary nature of external objects; then the imaginary character of the individual mind. Third, one will grasp the nondual nature of pure consciousness as neither existence nor nonexistence, neither affirmation nor negation, neither identity nor difference. At last even this state will be transcended and the state of liberation, wherein all categories are merged, will be reached.

Asat. From the Sanskrit which means "non-being" The opposite of "Sat" meaning "being." A theory of the origin of being from non-being dating back to Vedic times.

Asceticism. From the Greek askesis which means "self-denial." The veiw, which has been an important theme of both Eastern and Western religion and has played a minor role in philosophy, that the body is to be denied, possibly mortified, so as to make possible the purification of the soul in its progress toward salvation.

Ashramas, the Four. In the Mahabbharata and in Hinduism generally, the four stations of life, and their duties.

Ashvaghosa. 1st Century A.D.

Indian philosopher. The chief expounder of Mahayana Buddhism. Claiming that after Buddha's death there were many errors of interpretation among those who sought to understand his teachings, Ashvaghosa set out to explain the fundamental teachings of the Buddha.

Principal writings : The Awakening of the Faith in the Mahayana.

(1) Ashvaghosa holds that reality is "Absolute Suchness," that which it is, beyond the categories of human understanding.

(2) But the "Absolute Suchness," tainted by ignorance, appears as "Conditional Suchness," *i.e.*, as the manifold phenomenal world, including the apparent plurality of finite selves. In fact, as the calm water of the ocean, whipped by wind, appears as waves, so does consciousness, as the result of ignorance, appear as finite minds.

(3) The relative phenomenal world cannot be sublated by reason since this, too, is relative or relational. We must get beyond intellect and approach reality directly, and Buddha utilized words and definitions to lead the seeker beyond words and definitions.

(4) Following Buddha's example the bodhisattvas, those on the way to enlightenment, defer their own Nirvanas in order to enable others to overcome their ignorance, and so end their suffering.

(5) In the state of enlightenment we are aware of our Absolute Suchness and identify with the self existent immortal reality.

Asmita. A Sanskrit term which means "I am-ness." A false egoism which confuses the sensible self with the true self, or purusha. One of the five kinks of suffering to be overcome in the Yoga system.

Assertion Sign. The mark "⊢" introduced by Frege to distinguish between the mere stating or naming of a proposition, and holding it to be true. It was adopted by Russell and Whitehead in Principia Mathematica.

Assertoric. The term used for describing a proposition that simply asserts that something is or is not the case. The term has been used to contrast such proposition with modal propositions.

Assertoric Judgment. Refers to one of the three modes of judgment distinguished by Kant that one asserting that something is (or is not). The other two modes have been those of the Problematic judgment and the Apodeictic judgment. The analysis of modality goes back at least to Aristotle.

Association Of Ideas. A term introduced into philosophy by John Locke. The terms used for the view that complex mental phenomena are derived from the joining together of simple elements according to a small set of principles.

Associationism. Refers to a psychological rather than a philosophical theory, taking association to be the fundamental principle of mental life.

Association of Ideas. A psychologistic explanation advanced by Hume to refute certain philosophical "fictions", particularly in connection with the notion of causation.

Assumption. From the Latin ad ("to") and sumere ("take"). The taking for granted of the truth of a proposition for the sake of the argument.

ASTANGA YOGA. The eightfold path of discipline.

ASTIKA. Sanskrit term which means "orthodox." Any system of thought accepting the authority of the Vedas. To be contrasted to the Nastika system which do not accept their authority.

ASTIKAYA. Sanskrit term which means "physical." Used in Jainism in the phrase astikaya dravya or "physical substance." The term applied to matter, motion, rest, and space.

Ataraxia. The goal and inspiration of the Greek Sceptics. It was to be achieved by the clam and reasoned suspension of judgment (epoché) about contentious issues.

ATHARVA-VEDA. One of the four collections of hymns used in the Vedic sacrifices.

Atheism The rejection of belief in God, whether on the grounds that it is meaningful but false to say that God exists, or, as the logical positivists held, that it is meaningless and hence neither true nor false (logical positivism).

Atman. Sanskrit term which means "self" or "soul". In the Upanishads which means and in the Vedanta philosophy, Atman as the individual soul and Brahman, the ruler of all things, are held to be identical. Shankara gives one of the standard analyses of this identity.

Atomic Sentence. A sentence having no logical operator, and which is thus logically simple.

Atomic Uniformity, Principle of. The name given by J. M. Keynes to the further assumption, additional to that embodied in the principle of limited independent variety, supposedly required to justify induction: "the material universe must consist......of bodies.. such that each .. exercises its own separate, independent and invariable effect, a change of total state being compounded of a number of separate changes each of which is solely due to a separate portion of the preceding state".

Atomic Wff. A wff having no logical operator.

Atomism. The belief that matter consists of atoms. It is usually traced to the Greek philosophers. Leucippus and Democritus (5th century BC).

Attributive Denoting a particular placing of an adjective. The adjective 'white' is in the attributive position in 'Silver is a white horse' and in the predicative position in 'Silver, the horse, is white'.

Aufklarung. German term for Enlightenment.

Augustine of Hippo, St. 354-4 ( ). The greatest of the Latin Church fathers, born in North Africa. He studied and taught in Carthage, Rome, and Milan.

Although many passages in Augustine's work, like the famous analysis of time in the Confessions, suggest outstanding technical ability, his philosophy was almost always auxiliary to religious preoccupations. He saw both philosophy and religion as essentially quests for wisdom and, through wisdom, beatitude; the crucial difference was that Christian faith succeeded in the quest, while the unaided human reason of the philosophical schools could not. He did not, however, deny that some truths, including theological truths, were attainable by reason alone. Neoplatonism certainly helped him to break free from

Manichaean dualism, and Platonic concepts played an Important role in his interpretations of Christian teaching. But the task of reason was essentially that of elucidating things already accepted by faith as divine revelation—an attitude late summed up in the formula "Credo ut intelligam" (I believe so that I may understand).

Augustine's writings, especially on divine grace and the role and the authority of the Church, profoundly influenced both medieval and Reformation religious thought.

Aurobindo, Sri (Aurobindo Ghose). 1872-1950. Indian philosopher. A modern leader of the Advaita Vedanta philosophy in modern India, Aurobindo considered the illusionism of Shankara a misinterpretation of the Upanishads.

Principal writings : Essays on the Gita (E), 1926-44, 1950; The Life Divine (E), 2 vols., 1947; The Synthesis of Yoga (E), 1948 : The Supramental Manifestation upon Earth (E), 1952.

1. Reality exists in a graded series which begins in matter, and mounts to the Absolute itself, or Brahman. The essential power of Brahman requires his descent into the finite.

2. That same power requires the finite to struggle toward the infinite. On one level this struggle is the evolution of lower into higher forms. On another level man seeks, and must seek, identity with the Absolute by passing beyond the level of the mental into the divine life.

3. The means, of this passage is called 'integral yoya' providing a transformation of mind, life and body.

Authenticity. From the Greek authentes ("one who acts with authority, or what is done by one's own hand"). Anticipated in fiction by Goethe, the term has come into philosophic use with the existentialists, for whom it is an important value term.

Autological. A synonym for homological.

Autonomy. From the Greek autos ("self") and nomos ("law") Hence, the reference is to that which gives law to itself, or is its own law.

Autonomy of Ethics. Refers to the doctrine that the naturalistic fallacy is indeed a fallacy.

Avalokitesvara. The reincarnated Dalai Lama of Lamaism.

Avatar. From the Sanskrit avatara ("descent"). The term is used to refer to the descent of a deity to earth and his incarnation in man or animal. In Hinduism the term applies mainly to Vishnu. Nine avatars of the god have already appeared, and a tenth is expected.

Average. In one common sense, a word virtually synonymous with 'typical', 'ordinary,' or "in no way distinguished'. More technically, the average is the arithmetic mean.

Avesta. Avestan term which means "knowledge." The term applies to the sacred scriptures of the Zoroastrian religion.

Avicenna. (Arabic name: Ibn Sina abu' Ali al-Husayn). (980-1037). Islamic philosopher. Main works : Kitab al-Shifa' (The Book of Healing (of the Soul), abridged by Avicenna in Kitab al-Najat (The Book of Salvation), and Qanun fit 'l-Tibb (The Canon of Medicine). (The latter two works were printed in Rome in 1593).

Avidya. Sanskrit term which means "nescience" or "ignorance." A synonym is maya. Specifically, avidya is ignorance of t identity of self and Brahman in Indian philosophy, and therefore belief in the separate nature of self.

Avowals A term used by Ryle to describe certain first-person utterances (such as 'I am in pain') and to distinguish them from their thirdperson counterparts ('He is in pain').

Avyakta. From the Sanskrit meaning "unmanifest." A term used in the Upanishads and in the Bhagavad-Gita along with the term Prakriti to refer to the unmanifest power of God, or to Brahman before creation in the state of superabundance, or to the unborn universe.

Axiological Ethics. Refers to one of the types of ethics to be contrasted with deontological, teleological, intuitionistic, and formalistic types.

Axiology. Refers to the philosophical study of values, undertaken especially in the fields of ethics religion, and aesthetics.

Axiom. A statement for which no proof is required and which, thus, occurs as a premise of many arguments but as the conclusion of none.

Axioma. The term used by Ramus as the general name for statements. He distinguished axioma simplex, axioma generale, axioma particulara, and axioma proprium.

Axiomatic Method. Refers to a method of formalizing and studying a subject by using only the methods of formal logic in order to derive the truths of the subject from a list of underfined terms and a list of axioms.

Axiom of Infinity. An axiom of set theory that asserts, in one form or an other, that there exists a set with infinitely many members.

Ayam Atma Brahma. Sanskrit term which means "This self is Brahman."

B

Baal. Refers to a semitic term, *i.e*, one found in most Semitic languages, meaning "possessor". A title of divinity in the history of many Semitic peoples, baal signifies the possessor of a place, object, or attribute, but not a person. Deities of individuals and tribes bear other names, such as "Elohim".

Bad Faith. In the existentialism of Sartre, a form of deception of self and others; the attempt to rationalize human existence through religion, science, or any belief in operative forces that impose meaning and coherence. Man shapes his own destiny through a succession of free choices for which he is totally responsible. In 'bad faith' he denies the necessity of relying on his own moral insight and fallible will, trying to escape the burden of responsibility by regarding himself as the passive subject of outside influences, and his actions as being predetermined by these rather than freely chosen by himself.

Bahaism. A religious movement which was initiated by Baha u'llah, a schismatic Mohammedan who in the middle of the 19th century founded a new religion.

Baptism From the Greek baptein ("to dip in water"). The rite, religious or tribal, in which a liquid (usually water but sometimes oil, blood, urine, etc.) is applied to the human form by immersion, washing, pouring, or sprinkling, to ward off evil effects or purify from sin. The ritual has been world-wide, and is to be found in most religions. Baptism by water gained sacramental status in Roman Catholicism, and retains such status in most varieties of Protestantism.

Baptists. The term used for a major Protestant organization of congregational form, originating within English Congregationalism in the early 17th century, over the issue of the proper form of Baptism. Baptists stress the importance of personal religious experience. The denomination is having many subgroups within it.

Barber Paradox. A paradox which illustrates a problem in set theory. Suppose that the barber of Seville shaves all the men of Seville, except those who shave themselves. Does the barber shave himself? If he does shave himself, he is not to be shaved by the barber, that is, himself; if he doesn't he should be shaved by the barber. Hence he both does and does not shave himself. So the original supposition has been false.

Basic Action. Refers to a thing that we simply do without having to do anything else to make it happen. The contrast has been with those of our actions that involve causing things to happen (for example, exploding a demolition charge by pressing the detonator). Raising one's arm is the stock example of a basic action.

Basic Statements. A phrase which was coined by Ayer in the context of arranging the beliefs of an individual. If epistemology is conceived as the project of arranging the statements we believe according to the reasons we have for believing them, then we are likely, sooner or later, to come to beliefs for which no reason can be given.

Battle of Gods and Giants An image in Plato's Sophist describing the perennial conflict between two types of thinker : "One side drags down everything from heaven and the unseen to earth, rudely grasping rocks and trees in their hands For they get their grip on all such things, and they maintain that alone exists which can be handled and touched . Terrible men...Those who battle against them defend themselves very carefully from somewhere above in the unseen, contending that true existence consists in certain incorporeal Forms which are objects of the mind". Plato himself is the first forefather of the gods, Leucippus and Democritus, Hobbes and Marx, fight in the front line for the giants.

Beatification. From the Latin beatus ("blessed") and facere ("to make"). That stage in the Roman Catholic process of canonization whereby a candidate for sainthood is declared one of the "blessed" and entitled to public religious honor.

Beatific Vision. In Christianity the immediate vision of God which is enjoyed by the faithful in heaven.

Beauty. Refers to the sensible condition of aesthetic excellence considered to arouse the keenest pleasure.

Becoming. In philosophy, this term refers to the passage of events in time including the coming into being and going out of being of any quality. Process, orderly change, in contrast to changeless being.

Bedeutung. (German for : meaning). In the philosophical logic of Frege, the term standardly translated as 'reference' (compare Sinn).

Begging the Question. Refers to the procedure of taking for granted, in a statement or argument, precisely what is in dispute.

Behaviourism. The theory, first propounded by the psychologist J B. Watson in Behaviourism (1925), that psychological functioning has been definable in terms of observed behavioural data. Initially introduced in order to establish a firm scientific basis for psychology, the theory has since had extensive elaboration, notably in the writings of B.F. Skinner.

Being. From the Greek ousia and ontos; in Latin esse, essentia, and substantia are the basic referents to "being".

In philosophy the search for what underlies appearance led in Parmenides (q.v. 1-4) to the claim that "being is and non-being is not". For Parmenides being is changeless, rational, and one.

Being, the Great Chain Of. The phrase, used by A.O. Lovejoy as the title of his influential book, serve introduce a concept of importance running from Neoplatonism through the medieval period; that is, the concept of a graded reality embodying all of the possibilities in a continuum running from pure matter to pure spirit, from sheer potentiality to pure actuality.

Belief. Refers to the epistemic attitude of holding a proposition *p* to be true where there is some degree of evidence, through not conclusive evidence, for the truth of *p*. Clearly related to knowledge, belief may be characterized as stronger than mere ungrounded opinion but weaker than full knowledge. Importantly, while knowing *p* would generally be considered to entail, among other things, that *p* is true, believing *p* is consistent with the actual falsity of *p*.

Benevolence. From the Latin bene ("well") and volens ("wishing"). In philosophy a principle taken to support social interest and oppose self interest.

Bernoulli's Theorem. A concept in probability theory, also known as the law of large of numbers. Suppose that there is a sequence of n trials, on every one of which an outcome A is possible and on every one of which the probability of A is the same, say p. The theorem states that the probability that the proportion of As in the sequence lies within the range $p \pm h$ (where h is any small fraction) approaches 1 as n approaches infinity.

Berry's Paradox. Refers to an informal version of Richard's paradox.

Bertrand's Box Paradox. A paradox which suggests that different ways of describing alternatives lead to different probability assignments.

Bertrand's Paradox. A paradox which is illustrating difficulties in assigning probabilities where there are infinite alternatives.

Best, Principle of the. The Leibnizian principle of perfection, satirized by Voltaire in Candide through the hero's naive belief that "everything is for the best in the best of all possible words".

Bhagavad-Gita. From Sanskrit meaning the "Song of the Blessed". Title of the philosophical poem, in Book Six of the Mahabharata, an epic poem thought to date from the 6th century B.C. The poem is a dialogue between Arjuna, advancing into battle at the head of his family in opposition to a hostile family, and the God Krishna who acts as Arjuna's charioteer. The two families are rival claimants to the throne, and a principal part of the discussion is concerned with problems of ethics.

Bhairava. In Hinduism a name of Shiva meaning "fearful". The name of the third member of the Hindu trinity in his "fear" form. A dozen forms of this Bhairava-Shiva relationship are known, the most common being "Bhairava the Black" and "Bhairava the Dog".

Bhakti (Sanskrit for : devotion). In the vedanta and other Indian systems, love of God, expressed in prayer and meditation and ultimately in total self-surrender to the divine nature. Bhakti came to prominence during the medieval theistic period of

Indian thought; its philosophical basis was chiefly provided by Ramanuja (c. 1100 AD).

Bible. From the Greek biblia ("the books"), derived from the name of the Phoenician city, Byblos, an important source of papyrus. The term refers to the scriptures of the Jews (divided into the Law, Prophets and Writings) as well as to those of the Christians (39 books of the Old Testament and 27 of the New Testament).

Biblical Criticim. Refers to the application to the Bible of linguistic and historiographic tools in order to purify the text and provide a sound basis for its interpretation.

Biblicism. Refers to the adherence to the Bible as authoritative in a literal sense.

Biconditional. Refers to a statement in which it is asserted that possession of one property is a necessary and sufficient condition for possession of another, as in 'A number is prime iff it has no divisors other than one and itself, on that the existence of one state of affairs is a necessary and sufficient condition for the existence of another, as in 'He will be president iff he wins the election'.

Binary Operation. Refers to a two place operation.

Biology. From the Greek bios ('life') and logia ('knowledge of').

The study of biology was central to the Lyceum of Aristotle, and conducted on an experimental basis. Where the study of physics remained speculative and theoretical, knowledge of living forms was gained inductively and by dissection.

Bivalence, Principle (or law) of. Refers to the principle that states that every statement is either true or false; that is, that every statement has a truth value and that there are just two truth-values. In the presence of a negation operator, as standardly conceived, this principle entails that of the excluded middle, but since it makes no mention of negation is not equivalent to it. The law of excluded middle has been a logical law operating at the level of the object language, whereas the principle of bivalence is a semantic principle, one governing the interpretation of the language to which it is applied.

Bodhi A Sanskrit term which means "wisdom" or "enlightenment". Widely used in Indian philosophy, the term's opposite is avidya or ignorance.

Bodhidharma c. 460-c 534. The founder of Zen Buddhism.

Bodhisattva. In Sanskrit bodhi ('wisdom') and sattva ('existence in'). In Buddhism those who defer Buddhahood for the sake of others. The doctrine is to be found in both Hinayana and Mahayana Buddhism; but it is much more central to the latter.

Body. See Mind-Body Problem. For Descartes body is extended and has reference to space, time, and motion, standing in contrast to mind, which altogether lacks the first reference, retaining the third only in a metaphorical sense.

Boo-hooray Theory. Refers to the apt and widely employed nickname of the view of moral, and indeed of all evaluative, utterance expressed in Ayer's Language, Truth and Logic (1936). Such utterances, or the evaluative elements in them, do not state anything, but, like ejaculations, simply express the reactions of the speaker.

Book of Changes, the, (Or I Ching). Refers to one of the basic Chinese classics. The book arose in relation to the practice of divination, and was formed between the 6th and the 3rd centuries B.C. The book consists of sixty-four hexagrams, based on eight trigrams of three lines each. The trigram for heaven is— —. That for earth is ———. A divided line stands for the concept of Yin, an undivided line stands for Yang. The trigrams are combined into all the possible hexagrams, and are supposed to symbolize all possible situations. The hexagram formed by placing the trigram for water— —over the trigram for fire——— symbolizes conquest, triumph, oy success.

Book of the Dead. In Egyptian religion a book of formulae, prayers and hymns designed to assist the decreased in meeting the challenges of passage into the after-world.

Boolean Algebra. The algebra developed by Georage Boole (1815-64) as a way of manipulating symbols by purely algebraic methods (for example, multiplication), without regard for any particular interpretation but merely reflecting basic laws of thought. The term now refers to abstracts systems, similar in many respects to the original Boolean algebra, which may be applied to such diverse areas as probability and computer design.

Boundary Situation. From the German Grenzsituation, a term used to refer to those situations which set the limits of man's historical being, *i.e.*, death suffering, struggle, and guilt.

Boundless, The. Refers to a translation of the Greek apeiron. Underlying principle of change in the philosophy of Anaximander.

Brahma. Along with Vishnu and Shiva the Gods making up the Hindu trinity. Brahma is the Creator god.

Brahman. Sanskrit term, etymology uncertain. The term may have meant 'magic,' referring to the gaining of magical results through ritual and sacrifice.

Brahmins. The ruling class in Indian tradition

Brutes. All animals other than man. A famous passage in Descartes' Discourse deals with 'the difference between men and brutes.' The crucial point about animals, for Descartes, is their lack of language : animal 'utterances' are always elicited by a specific stimulus and never amount to genuine speech.

Buddha, Gautama Siddhartha, 560-477 B.C. Founder of the Buddhist faith. Born in South Nepal India, in the foothills of the eastern Himalayas. Son of a king of the Shakya clan. He is said to have made the great renunciation after the birth of his first child.

Buddhism. The religion founded by Gautama Buddha in the 6th century B.C. Arising in the Eastern provinces, far from the Indus Valley, center of Vedic culture.

Buddhism, Hinayana. 400-250 B.C. (Formative period). The earlier and more strict of the two interpretations of Buddhism which arose after Gautama Buddha's death. The term 'Hinayana" means "the small vehicle" and was given to this variant form by its chief rival which was self-styled as "Mahayana" or the great vehicle."

Buddhism, Mahayana. 0-500 A.D. (Formative period). The later, more popular and more elaborate of the two interpretations of Buddhism which arose after the death of the founder, Gautam, Buddha. Members of the movement gave themselves the name 'Mahayana' meaning 'the great vehicle.' To be contrasted with the term 'Hinayana' meaning 'the small vehicle' which they applied to the earlier and more strict interpretation of the teachnigs of Buddha.

Buddhist Councils. Two councils are acccepted by all Buddhists, and three by most. The first was a seven-month session held in 483 B.C. following Buddha's death.

Buddhist Philosophy. Buddhism is an originally Indian religion, founded in the 5th century BC by Siddhartha Gautama, the 'Buddha' (enlightened one).

Burali-Forti's Paradox. The paradox of the greatest ordinal, and one of the logical paradoxes.

Buridan's Ass. The traditional illustrative example, first found in Aristotle but now associated with Buridan, of the problem of decision making when there is no reason for preferring one of the possible alternatives. The ass, faced with two equally desirable haybales, starves to death through indecision since, ex hypothesi, there are no grounds for preferring one bale to the other.

Bushido. From the Japanese bushi ('warrior') and ('way' or 'principle'). The term refers to the chivalric code (Confucian and Zen. Buddihst in origin) of the warrior-knight in feudal Japan.

Byzantine Church. In a strict sense those congregations falling under the jurisdiction of the Church of Constantinople. In a looser sense the entire group of Eastern Orthodox Churches.

C

Cabala. The term is employed to designate a set of mystical doctrines which developed within Judaism between the last pre-Christian centuries and the 14th century, and the collection of books written in support of these doctrines. The Cabala developed in contrast to orthodox Jewish doctrine, emphasizing exactly the elements rejected by the orthodox.

Calculus. Refers to a system of symbols so organized that inferences can be made by manipulating the symbols of the system according to rule. The elements of any calculus : have been symbols, definitions, axioms, and rules of inference. Some of these symbols must be primitive, or underfined; the rest will be defined in terms of those which are undefined. Through the appropriate combination of symbols, well formed formulae and, through the mainpulation of such formulae, the theorems of the calculus, can be gained.

Calemes. Valid syllogism in AEE mood, fourth figure.

Callicles. 5th century B.C.A Greek philosopher and politician, Callicles enters Plato's dialogue, Gorgias, as one of Socrates' contemporaries. One of the Sophists, he argues that the natural law by which the strong rule is also a natural right and an expression of natural justice. The conventions of society attempt to enslave the strong and thus subvert natural justice. He also argues for pleasure as the goal of life.

Calvinism. Refers to the movement of thought and practice following from Calvin's work.

Cambridge Platonists. An English intellectual movement centering in Cambridge University in the third quarter of the 17th century. Centering around problems in the philosophy of religion, the group stood largely in the tradition of Neoplatonism, citing especially Plato, Proclus, and Plotinus. Jacob Boehme, Descartes, and Malebranche also received attention.

Canon. A Latin term which means "measuring line", "rule", or "model", derived from the Greek kanon ("rule" or "rod").

(1) Canons of scripture are those writings regarded as authoritative for a given religion. The Jewish or Hebrew canon consists of the Law, Prophets, and Writings. The Christian canon, or Bible consists of 39 books of the Old Testament and 27 of the New.

(2) Canon Law. The most authoritative law of the Roman Catholic Church, bearing the authority of Scripture, pope, or council. To be distinguished from decrees of bishops, church-state concordats, and church law resting on custom. The body of Canon Law was published in 1582 by Gregory XIII as the Corpus Juris Canonici. A new codification, known as the Codex Juris Canonici, was promulgated under Benedict XV in 1917.

Canonization. In Roman Catholicism the decree placing a person in the catalogue or canon of saints and commending that he be venerated. Necessary to canonization is the prior achievement of beatification and the authentication of at least two miracles by intercession of the person, always deceased, under consideration.

Cantor's Paradox. Refers to a paradox in set theory which was discovered by Georg Cantor. The paradox is generated by the question of whether the set of all sets has been (a) equal to or (b) greater than its own power set. If (a), a contradiction arises in that it can be proved that the power set of any given set is greater than the set itself. If (b), a contradiction arises since the power set of any set is itself a set of sets and therefore a subset of the set of all sets, and it can be proved that the subset of any given set is not greater than the given set.

Capitalism. Refers to that economic system which stresses the role of capital, *i.e.*, wealth of all sorts including economic goods utilized in the production of other goods.

(1) The classical expression of capitalism is credited to Adam Smith who argued for the free play of a self-regulating market and who believed that, given competition, the operation of an "invisible hand" would move prices to "natural" levels and induce labor and capital to move from less to more profitable enterprises. In sort, man's competitive strivings would be transmuted automatically into the common good.

(2) The French term laissez-faire ("let do" or "let make"), derived from the Physiocrats (q.v.), came to be attached to "capitalism" as a qualifying phrase. The total phrase "laissez-faire capitalism" emphasized the point that in this system economic interests where to be let alone to continue their development without government control and with a minimum of regulation.

(3) Mex Weber found the rise of capitalism and that of Protestantism to be related, the former standing as a secularized version of the latter's emphasis on individualism, and the necessity that one work out his own salvation.

Cardinality. The cardinality of a set, X, refers to any property possessed by all and only those sets equivalent to X. (Two sets are equivalent iff members of one set can be paired off with members of the other set in such a way that each member of either set is paired with exactly one member of the other, that is, there is a one-to-one correspondence between members of the two sets.) The set of all those sets equivalent to X is sometimes taken as a cardinal number. Intuitively, two sets share the same cardinality iff they have the same number of members.

Cardinal Virtues. A term introduced by St. Ambrose, having come across Plato's classification of the natural virtues in the writings of Cicero.

(1) Among the Greeks, and for Plato, the virtues were "wisdom", "courage", "temperance" and "justice".

(2) Among the Scholastics the cardinal virtues were seven in number. They included the foregoing, termed natural virtues, and three additional "theological" virtues: "faith", "hope", and "charity".

(3) Geulincx held the cardinal virtues to be diligence, obedience, justice, and humility.

Cartesian. Of or relating to Rene Descartes.

Carvaka. See Indian materialism.

Cartesianism. From Renatus Cartesius, the Latinized form of the name of Rene Descartes. The term refers to all philosophies inspired by the methods and assumptions of Descartes.

Casualism. From the Latin casus ("tall", "accident"). Taken literally, although the usage tends to be obsolete, the doctrine that all things result from chance.

Casuistry. In ethics, this term refers to the systematic discussion of the applicability of general moral laws to particular cases of conduct, accommodating new ideas that enter and challenge social order.

Catechism. From the Greek katexein ("teach by word of mouth"). A compendium of essential religious instruction arranged in the form of questions and answers. Although it is common to many religions, in Western usage the term refers to practices of Jewish Eastern Orthodox, Roman Catholic, and Protestant religious instruction.

Categorematic. In traditional logic, this term denotes a word that can stand on its own as a term (either a subject or a predicate) in a categorical proposition. In modern logic, its meaning has been extended to include any symbol that has independent meaning, for example 'red', 'animal', 'Aristotle'. Compare syncategorematic.

Categorical Imperative. A term which was introduced into ethics by Kant to distinguish the guidance to action given by morality that of other forms of prescription.

Category From the Greek kategoria, composed of kata ("against") and agoreuein ("to assert"). The term came to mean an assertion, or predication, and then "an ultimate concept or form of thought" or "a major form of predication."

Category Mistake. Refers to a notion, prominent in Ryle's philosophy, depending upon one or another theory of categories. It is namely, a category mistake. It represents the facts of mental life as if they belonged to one logical type of category (or range of types or categories) when they actually belong to another".

Catharsis. From the Greek katharsis ("purification"). Aristotle held that the function of tragedy is a purging of the viewer's emotion's of pity and fear.

Causa. Latin term which means "cause". Among Latin phrases embodying the term the following have to be noted. Causa cognoscendi refers to the cause of our knowledge of an event, and has to be distinguished from causa essendi, the cause of the event itself.

Casual Theory of Perception. The theory used for the view that, although we can never be directly acquainted with more than the veil of appearance, materials things can nevertheless be known as the hypothesized causes of our sense data.

Causa Sui. (Latin for: cause of itself or himself.) An expression which is applied mainly to God, by those who, while insisting that God cannot have been produced by or be dependent on anything else are nevertheless reluctant to say that God is uncaused.

Causation. Refers to the relationship between two events or states of affairs such that the first brings about the second.

Cause. From Latin causa. A term correlative to the term "effect". That which occasions, determines, produces, or conditions an effect; or is the necessary antecedent of an effect.

Cave, Image of The. Plato's illustration in the Republic (Book VII) of the difference between knowledge and illusion, reality and appearance. Men chained in a cave, facing a blank wall, with a fire burning behind them, can only shadows, which they take for real objects.

Certainty. From the Latin cernere and the Greek krinein ('to decide').

(1) Logical certainty is a property of valid conclusions in deductive inference (q.v. Logic), the property being simply that the conclusion follows necessarily from the premises. Since one is interested in true conclusions, however, it is necessary to have true premises as well as valid reasoning.

(2) Psychological certainty is a state of belief in the truth or falsity of a given proposition; and this state does not insure truth in one's conclusions, even should the latter be gained by valid reasoning.

Certainty and Doubt. Concepts that play an important part in Cartesian theory of knowledge. In the first of his Meditations, Descartes argued that if one is to know that a proposition *p* is true, then (a) one must be certain that *p*, and (b) one must be unable to doubt that *p*. So if one is to say, with justification, 'I know that *p*', one must not be in a position in which one may at some time have to take back one's assertion that *p*; the assertion that *p* must be such that one cannot doubt the truth of what one says.

Ceteris Paribus. Latin phrase which means 'other things being equal.'

Chabarites. An Islamic school of thought espousing absolute fatalism.

Chain of Being. A metaphor for the order, unity, and completeness of the created world, thought of as a chain extending to include all possibilities of existence, from God to the tiniest particle of inanimate matter.

Change. Refers to the opposite of permanence, and one of the basic categorials ideas.

(1) Heraclitus held to the universality of constant change, explaining that it takes place by opposites. His example was the tension of the drawn bow.

(2) Parmenides, Zeno and Nagarjuna argued for permanence and against the possibility of change.

(3) Aristotle distinguished three types of change : alteration, growth or diminution, and locomotion.

(4) Bergson and Whitehead made the category of becoming or process central to their philosophies.

Chaos. The term first used in the Theogony of Hesiod (8th century BC) to describe the gap resulting from the separation of heaven and earth during the emergence of the world from an undifferentiated state; it was interpreted by Aristotle as the pre-philosophic concept of space.

Character Complex. The term for "sense-datum" (q.v.), employed in the movement of Critical Realism.

Charismata. From the Greek charisma ("gift"). In early Christianity the term applied to the "gifts of the Spirit," especially the gift of "speaking the tongues." Paul carefully broadened the application of the term, insisting that love is the very highest charisma.

Ch'i. In early Chinese philosophy the term associated with the psychophysiological state of possessing the attributes of life. Subsequently it was contrasted with the Neo-Confucian concept of li.

Charvaka. Indian philosophical system of Materialism, traceable to the Rig Veda. Its principal development came in 600 B.C. in the no longer extant Brhaspati Sutra. The doctrine of Materialism, called Lokayata, has had many adherents since that time.

(1) The principles of all things are earth, air, fire, and water.

(2) That which cannot be perceived does not exist; to exist is to be perceivable.

(3) Intelligence is only body disposed in a certain manner and the soul is only the body as distinguished by intelligence.

(4) The only end of man is the enjoyment of sensual pleasure, and the avoidance of pain. Heaven and hell are the inventions of stupid men.

(5) The practice of religion has its sufficient explanation in providing a good living for the priests, and the authors of the Vedas were "buffoons, knaves, and demons."

(6) Even so-called universal ideas and relations are to be understood through perceptual connections, reinforced by memory. And this feature reduces the power of inference.

(7) The connection of cause and effect must be understood perceptually, also, and when we do so, its basis disappears for we may perceive the two horns of a cow successively and one horn would not seem to be the cause of the other.

(8) Finally, neither the existence nor non-existence of anything can be firmly established.

Chiliasm. From the Greek term chiliad which means "thousand." The millenarian doctrine that Christ would soon return to initiate a thousand-year reign on earth prior to the end of time.

Chinese 'Logicians' The. A 4th-century B.C. school of philosophers carrying the traditional Chinese concern with rectification of names in the direction of logical analysis. One of the smallest of the schools, the Logicians were without influence after their own-time. Hui Shih and Kung-Lung were the school's most noted thinkers.

Chinese Philosophy. 6th cent. B.C. to the Present. Until recent years the factors related in the philosophical history of this culture have been Confucianism, Taoism, Moism, the Logicians, Legalism, the Y in Yang School, and Chinese Buddhism.

Choice. Axiom Of. An axiom of set theory. Given any set X, the members of which are non-empty disjoint sets (that is, no two member sets of X have any members in common and each member set has at least one member), the axiom of choice states that there exists a (choice) set that consists of exactly one member of each of the members of X. The axiom has been shown to be independent of the other axioms of set theory.

Christ, Jesus. 4 B.C. -29. A.D. Founder of the, Christian religion. Born in Bethlehem; childhood in Nazareth. Began his ministry at the age of or ate thirty thirty-two. His ministry lasted, then, one to three years. On charges of blasphemy and sedition he was tried and executed on the authority of Rome.

Church. Interpretation of the nature of the Christian Church, including its relation to the state, varies with the branch or denomination of Christianity under consideration. Reference should thus be made to Catholicism, Protestantism, Lutheranism etc. for such considerations. Among specific references to the Church, however, we include the following :

(1) John Huss defined the Church as "the body of the predestinate."

(2) Sebastian Franck declared allegiance to the "church universal" rather than to any specific church.

(3) Hooker viewed church and state as aspects of the same government with the power of the state extending over the church.

(4) Pufendorf held that the supreme jurisdiction of religious matters rests in the state, while ecclesiastical power resides in the Church.

(5) Gioberti looked upon the Church as the consummation of the ideal of perfection, and hence essential to man's well-being on earth.

Church's Theorem. The theorem stated in 1936 by Alonzo Church to the effect that there is no algorithm for the first order functional calculus or any stronger theory, such as arithmetic.

Citta. Sanskrit term which means "mind stuff." A key term in the interpretation of the ego in the Yoga system.

Civilization. Often regarded as synonymous with "culture". Spengler distinguished between the two, finding civilization the final stage in a society's development. Alfred Weber distinguished between the "civilization process" and the "culture process," regarding the former as continuous and the latter as sporadic.

Class. From the Latin classis. There is no single all-encompassing term in Greek. Any multiplicity of entities sharing a common characteristic. The idea of classes arose in the development of logic, and is present in all major cultures.

The Code of Manu. An Indian metrical work of 2,685 verses concerned with the development of the orthodox Brahmànical view in relation to religion, law, custom, and politics.

(1) Supporting the four orders (or ashramas) of life—student, householder, hermit, and ascetic—the life of the householder, supporting the other three, is declared to be best. But man should pass through all four stages. The third, designed to loosen the bonds of life, requires retirement to the forest for mediation in preparation for the final stage in the attempt to gain enlightenment.

(2) The duties of the four castes are outlined : Brahmins—teaching, studying, performing sacrifices, accepting gifts from pure men. Kshatriyas—protection of the order of society, including the caste system. Vaisyas—attention to the details of agriculture and trade. Sudras—servile labor for one of the higher castes; and if this service is given a Brahmin the Sudra is promised birth into a higher caste in his next existence.

(3) Women are to be honored, but kept in dependence by the males of their families—by father, then husband, and finally, by sons. A faithful wife will share the fate of her husband beyond this life.

(4) The most virtuous and efficacious act is to be recognize the self in all created beings.

Clock Paradox. A paradox that arises from the special theory of relativity, which predicts that clocks run more slowly in a frame of reference moving at speeds approaching the velocity of light when observed from a stationary frame of reference. Thus, if one of a pair of twins embarks on a high-speed space journey, he will, when he returns be younger than his brother who has remained on earth. The resolution to this form of the paradox is that the departure, turn-around, and return of the space-travelling twin involve accelerations and decelerations, which are not covered by the special theory.

Clocks, Image of the Two. An illustration provided by Geulincx, and later used by Leibniz in presenting his own response to the Cartesian mind body problem. If two clocks are seen to keep perfect time with each other, there are three ways that this could arise :

(1) through mutual influence;

(2) through constant adjustments by the mechanic who cares for them;

(3) through their own inbuilt individual exactitude.

If one substitutes mind for one clock and body for the other, the three ways of agreement become three possible responses to the Cartesian problem :

(1) two way interactionism;

(2) occasionalism; and

(3) Leibniz's own preferred solution, harmonious parallel functioning.

Cogito Ergo Sum (Latin for : I think; therefore I am.) The most common formulation of the Cartesian argument for the basic certainty of one's own existence.

Cognition. From the Latin cognitio ('knowledge' or 'recognition'). the term refers both to the act or process of knowing and to knowledge itself. Competing theories of knowledge are the subject matter of epistemology. Cognition involves perception, memory, institution, and judgment.

Cognitive

1. Denoting mental processes which are connected with understanding, formulation of beliefs, and acquisition of knowledge, and thus distinct from volitional processes, such as wanting or intending.

2. Denoting utterances that are both significant and either true or false, in contrast to other utterances, such as commands and exclamations, that are significant and intelligible but cannot be classed as either true or false (sometimes called 'non-cognitive').

Cognitive Achievement Word. A word that, when used correctly in a claim about a proposition (or an object) entails the truth of that proposition (or the existence of the object).

Cognoscendum. From the Latin cognoscere ('to know'). Any object of a cognition whether veridical, fictive, abstract, or ideal.

Coherence Theory of Truth. A theory of the nature of truth which is associated with objective idealism. It states that truth is essentially system, by which is meant that the progress of knowledge is a progress towards a single complete system of thought, and that truth is predicable of this system alone.

Coincidentia Oppositorum. Latin phrase which means "coincidence of opposites", a principle utilized by Nicholas of Cusa.

Collective. In von Mises' treatment of probability, an infinite sequence of elements some of which correspond to a certain attribute or result, and which satisfies the conditions of convergence and randomness.

Collective Unconscious. In the psychology of C.G. Jung, the inherited unconscious, that contains the "archetypes", the symbolic epitomes of the experience of the whole human species.

Collectivism. Another name for political holism.

Colligation. From the Latin col ("together") and ligare ("to bind").

(1) For Whewell the placing of isolated information under a general conception. The manner in which an elliptical orbit organized separate observations of planetary position was cited by Whewell as an example of colligation.

(2) J.S. Mill pointed out that every instance of induction is colligation, although some instances of colligation, *e.g.*, those involved in immediate or intuitive knowledge, may not be induction.

(3) Peirce held the term to its literal meaning and associated the term with deduction rather than induction, holding that in deduction one colligates premises, and then determines what can be derived from them.

Combinatory Logic. An approach to logic substituting function symbols for variables.

Common Consent Arguments. Arguments from the (almost) universal acceptance of a belief, especially belief in God, to the truth of that belief. Apart from difficulties of determining how nearly universal belief in God has been throughout human history, or what should count as such belief, any argument of the form "(Almost) everyone believes *p*, therefore *p* is true" is clearly invalid.

Common Notions. From the Latin notions communes. This in turn is Cicero's translation of the Greek phrase koinai ennoiai, used by the Stoic philosophers. The concept held that all men possess a common set of basic ideas serving as the starting point of knowledge (q.v. Stoicism 1).

Common Sense

1. In general, the kind of opinions about life at large (for example, that the world has existed for a long time or that our minds are incorporeal) that philosophers believe unphilosophical people take for granted.
2. (in Aristole) The faculty that integrated the data of the five senses into unified apprehensions of objects.

Common Sense Realism. The view that we are able to perceive the external world directly, and that sense-data Sense-datum) either do not exist or play a subordinate role in perception.

Communism. From the Latin communis ('common'. 'universal', 'public'). A social structure where all things are held in common. According to Aristotle, communism was first advanced by Phaleas of Chalcedon and Hippodamus of Miletus.

Commutation The logical or mathematical operations whose result remains unchanged although the sequence of operations is changed. Many arithmetical and algebraic operations are commutative. Conjunction, disconjunction, equivalence, and many other operations are commutative in the Propositional Calculus and in the algebra of classes there are comparable operations.

Complete. Denoting, very roughly, a formal system in which the rules and axioms of the system allow one to construct enough proofs (axiom; proof). But what counts as 'enough' may be judged relative to different purposes, and there are a variety of non-equivalent requirements giving rise to non-equivalent notions of completeness.

Completeness. Along with Dedicability and Consistency one of the basic concepts of contemporary metalogic. A calculus or system is complete when :

(1) each of its wellformed formulae, or their negates, is a theorem of the calculus; or

(2) when any wellformed formula can either be proved in the system or else introduces inconsistency into it.

Composition and Division. There are two different ways in which the terms 'composition' and 'division' are used, and different fallacies are associated with each. The first is concerned with the reference of terms used in an argument; the second with changes of meaning obtained by different combinations of terms.

Compossibility. A Leibnizian principle of coherence defining a possible world, and the possible co-existence of its contents.

Comprehension. A term used by John Stuart Mill to signify what is usually called Intension.

Conatus. From Latin conani meaning to attempt. The term refers to endeavor. In Spinoza's philosophy all things are animated by conatus, the desire to perpetuate their being.

Concept. From the Latin con ("together" and capere (to seize or tame'). An idea as distinguished from a percept or sensation.

Conceptualism The theory of universals according to which general or abstract terms (such as 'substance' or 'humanity') have meaning because they name or otherwise refer to corresponding non-physical entities, called concepts. In the most substantial, but perhaps last plausible view, these concepts are taken to be mental images.

Conciliar Movement. A movement within the Roman Catholic Church asserting the authority of councils in church matters.

Concrete Universal. A term used in Hegelian philosophy to encapsulate Hegel's view that thinking must be universal (that is, in terms of universal law), but not abstractly universal.

Conditional

(1) (adj) Describing a statement in which it is claimed that something is, or will be, the case, provided that, or on the condition that, some other situation obtains.

(2) (n) A conditional or hypothetical statement. Such statements are characteristically expressed using the word 'if.

Conditional Statement. In the Propositional Calculus (q.v. 19) the name given to the binary connection 'if,..then', often symbolized by the horseshoe, '⊃' 'If it rains, then the streets will be wet' would be written 'it rains⊃the streets will be wet' The general form of the connection is 'p⊃q.' The truth table for the conditional statement shows statements of this sort to be true in all save the case where the antecedent is true and the consequent false.

Configurationism. The English term occasionally used for Gestalt theory.

Confirmation. The relation between propositions when one supports or adds credence to another. Confirmation theory hopes to delimit what kind of proposition or theory is confirmable (that is, capable of gaining support from experience), this being a necessary task of any kind of positivism.

Confucianism. Philosophy of the school founded by Confucius (551 – 479 BC), whose name in its familiar Western form is a Latinization of Chinese K'ung fu-tzu 'Venerable Master K'ung'.

Congregationalism. A Protestant movement, originating in England in the late 16th and 17th centuries, with the goal of either purifying (the Puritans) or separating from (the Separatists) the Established Church.

Congruism. The doctrine that grace leads the elect to yield themselves to God congruently with their own free will.

Connotation. From the Latin con ('with') and notare ('to note or mark')). The word thus refers to the group of characteristics or qualities essential to a term. The usual correlate of connotation is 'denotation the set of things to which the term refers. Intension signification and comprehension are often treated as synonymous with 'connotation.

Conscience. The holding of a conviction that some action is morally obligatory (or wrong) and to be firmly committed to doing (or refraining from doing) it. Those who consider that all moral beliefs provide overriding reasons for acting thereby make them all matters of conscience.

Consciousness. A term with two related philosophical uses : first, as for example, for Locke, in the sense of self-knowledge acquired by virtue of the mind's capacity to reflect upon itself in introspective acts analogous with perception; and second, in a broader modern sense, opposed to anaesthesia, designating what is held to be the general property of mental states.

Consensus Gentium. Latin phrase meaning "the agreement of mankind".

Consequence. If S is a set of statements, the statement A is said to be a consequence of S if the truth of A follows from the joint truth of members of S. The force of 'follows form' may be interpreted in various ways, each interpretation giving rise to a different consequence relation.

Consequential Characteristics. An alternative name for supervenient characteristics.

Consequentialism. An umbrella term for any moral theories that state that the rightness or wrongness, goodness or badness of an action is solely dependent on the results the action produces.

Consistency. From the Latin con ("with") and sistere ("to stand" or "cause to stand"). The characteristic, then, of being capable of standing together, or in harmony.

Consistent and Inconsistent. A set of statements is inconsistent if it entails a contradiction or has contradictory consequences, and is consistent otherwise. The bifurcation of the notion of consequence into semantic and syntactic notions creates a corresponding division between notions of consistency.

Constant. From the Latin con ("to") and stare ("stand"). Hence, the quality of standing firm.

Constative. A term which was coined by J.L. Austin to refer to an utterance with which one makes a true or false statement. It was initially contrasted with performative.

Constructivism. Refers to the view that mathematical entities exist only if they can be constructed (or, intuitively, shown to exist), and that mathematical statements are true only if a constructive proof can be given. It is thus opposed to any view of mathematics—for example, platonism that sees mathematical objects and truths existing or being true independently of (our) apprehension.

Consubstantiation. From the Latin con ("with") and substantia ("substance"). The Lutheran doctrine of the Eucharist to the effect that the body and blood of Christ are "in real substantial presence" with the bread and wine.

Contemplation. From the Latin con and templum (a space set aside for the observation and interpretation of signs and portents). Although the interpretation of the term has changed, its religious origin has not been entirely lost. The interpretation of theoria, or theory, in Greek philosophy, merely enlarged it with a truth-related aspect.

Contextualism. A theory of aesthetic interpretation that holds that a work of art should be understood in its total cultural context, and that every work is historically conditioned.

Contiguity. Togetherness in time or place. A basic principle of the Association of Ideas.

Contingency

(1) (of entities) The property of not having to exist.

(2) (of events) The property of not having to occur.

(3) (of propositions) The property of not having to be true, or of risking the possibility of being false.

Continuity. From the Latin continere, meaning "to hold together". The problem of continuity arises whenever one is concerned with series or fields. It arises, therefore, with respect to numbers, lines, planes, and solids.

Continuum. The concept of a reality, or a dimension of reality, without breaks, thus exemplifying continuity.

Continuum Problem. The problem of how many subsets of natural numbers there are; equivalently, of how many real numbers, that is, points on the continuum, there are.

Contradictio in Adjecto. From the Latin meaning a "contradiction in what is added'. A logical fallacy wherein there is a contradiction between the noun and adjective of a descriptive phrase, *e.g.* a dimensionless area.

Contradiction. A simultaneous assertion and denial of one and the same proposition occurring within or between contentions, assumptions, suppositions, and other forms of assertive discourse.

Contradiction, Principle (or law) **Of.** A logical principle, which in Aristotle's formulation, states that 'The same attribute cannot at the same time belong and not belong to the same subjected and in the same respect'.

Contradictory

1. (adj) Describing a discourse containing contradictions.
2. (n) Either of two propositions so related that both cannot be true or both cannot be false. Thus the proposition 'It is not the case that p' (symbolized as-p, and read 'not p') is the contradictory of the proposition p, and the other way about.

Contraposition. Refers to a valid form of immediate inference in which a conditional or universal statement appears as premise and its contrapositive as conclusion.

Contrapositive. Refers to the contrapositive of the conditional statement 'If p, then q' is 'If not -q, then not -p' and of a universal statement 'All As are B' is 'All non-Bs are non-A'.

Contrary. Either of two propositions so related that both may be false but only one can be true.

Contrary-to-fact Conditional. A counterfactual conditional.

Conventionalism. The view that scientific laws are disguised conventions reflecting the decision to adopt one of various possible descriptions.

Converse

1. (in Aristotelian logic). The proposition derived by conversion of the original. The converse of 'No S are P is 'No P are S' and of 'Some S are P' is 'Some P are S'. Conversion in both these cases is called simple conversion. The converse of 'All S are P' is 'Some P are S' and the inference in this case is called conversion per accidens. 'Some S are not P' has no converse.
2. (in propositional logic) The converse of a conditional statement 'If p then q' is 'If q then p'. In this case the converse is not a logical consequence of the original.

Converse Fallacy of the Accident. The mistake of arguing from a qualified principle, or a particular case (such as, it is never wrong to kill in order to save your own life), to an unqualified or general principle (such as, it is never wrong to kill). The (rarer) error of arguing from a general rule to a particular case without taking account of factors (accidents) that vitiate the rule is known as the fallacy of the accident. Both fallacies are sometimes known by their Latin scholastic tag secundum quid.

Conversion. Refers to a form of immediate inference in which the order of the terms is reversed.

Copula. From the Latin co ('together') and apere ('to bind). In traditional logic, a form of the verb 'to be' (plus 'not' in negative proposition) connecting the subject and predicate terms of a proposition.

Corpuscularian. An obsolete synonym for 'atomic', used particularly in the 17th century in connection with the philosophy of Gassendi, Boyle, and Locke.

Corpus Hermeticum. A body of Neoplatonic, astrological, and alchemical writings falsely supposed to drive from the Egyptian equivalent of the Greek and Hermes. The position of Hermetism which came from this material was of influence in the late Greek and Roman periods.

Correspondence Theory of Truth. Considered in its widest sense, the claim that truth is agreement with reality—that it consists in a correspondence between (for example) a statement and 'the way things are'.

Corroboration. A notion introduced by Karl Popper in The Logic of Scientific Discovery to replace that of confirmation in the process of testing scientific hypotheses.

Cosmogony. A scientific or mythic account of the origin of the Universe. Among primitive races, a cosmogony is portrayed as a single act of creation in time, with the world emerging or being shaped from one, or a few very simple, principles or elements.

Cosmological Argument. One of the three standard arguments for God, along with the teleological and ontological arguments.

Cosmology. The branch of philosophy, often considered a subdivision of metaphysics, that deals with the Universe as a totality of phenomena, attempting to combine metaphysical speculation and scientific evidence within a coherent framework.

Cosmos. The Pythagorean notion of the world as a rational ordered whole. The Greek word implies fitness and beauty as well as orderedness within finite limits.

Counter-example. An instance of the kind of thing over which a generalization or universal statement has been made, which lacks the property said to be possessed by all things of that kind.

Counterfactual Statement. A conditional statement whose antecedent is false and whose consequent is conditionally true.

Count Noun. A term standing for an item in a countable class. Thus, girls being countable, 'girl' is a count noun

Courage. From the Latin cor ('heart'). One of the four Greek cardinal virtues along with wisdom, temperance, and justice.

Covenant. In religious parlance a formal agreement entered into between man and God.

Covering Law Model. Refers to the model that represents explanation as a matter of finding a law that covers, in the sense of entailing, the phenomenon to be explained.

Craig's Theorem. The proof, provided by William Craig in 1953, that if we axiomatize a scientific theory formally and partition the vocabulary into two parts (one supposedly 'theoretical' and the other 'observational'), then there will be an axiomatization from which all the sentences involving only observational terms are deducible and which itself contains none of the theoretical terms.

Creation. The action required both to produce the Universe out of nothing and to be its indispensible sustaining cause.

Creationism. The doctrine that God creates a soul for every human being.

Creativity. A process resulting in novelty stressed by some philosophers :

(1) Freud gave an analysis of personal creativity in terms of sublimation and emergence of the sublimated in a novel form.

(2) Whitehead held that creativity is the Category of the Ultimate, and that the universe is involved from moment to moment in a creative advance.

(3) Lossky regarded creativity as the essential characteristic of both God and man.

(4) Berdyaev likewise stressed self-creation as characterizing man and God. In his analysis it is in both cases creation out of nothing.

(5) Wieman has centered on the creative event, consisting of four sub-events, and resulting in 'creative good.' He identifies the creative event with God.

Credo. Latin for 'I believe.' A creed or confession of faith. A number of Latin phrases beginning with 'credo' have been used as slogans by theologians and by some philosophers.

Creed. From the Latin credo ('I believe.') A doctrinal formula accepted by a religious group as binding. Creeds have been elaborated in many religions, invariably arising from situations containing disagreement or danger, for the sake of insuring unity among believers.

Criterion. From the Greek krinein ('to judge, discern'). The rule or body of rules by which decisions may be reached on the truth or falsity of judgments. Thus, the problem of the criterion usually relates to Epistemology.

Critical Idealism. Another name for Kant's transcendental idealism.

Critical Realism. The doctrine accepted by some philosophers sympathetic to the view of R.W. Sellars, as published in Critical Realism (1916). Critical realism retains the belief of common-sense realism in independent physical things, but admits that these are not directly and homogeneously presented to us in perceptual situation. These latter are thought to be very various, and our understanding of them must depend in part on the state and findings of the natural sciences.

Criticism. From the Greek krinein ('to judge, discern').

(1) In philosophy the term applies most directly to the critical philosophy of Immanuel Kant as reflected in his Critique of pure Reason, Critique of Practical Reason, and Critique of Judgement. Kant's object was to investigate the nature and limits of human understanding.

(2) In religion one must distinguish textual criticism (aimed at producing an authentic text) from higher criticism (fitting the text into its historical context). Spinoza (q.v.) is regarded as one of the forerunners of higher criticism (in his Tractatus or Theological-Political Treatise).

Culture. From the Latin colere meaning 'to till or cultivate'. The term is sometimes used to include all of the creative expressions of man in all fields of human endeavor. At other times it is confined to creative expression in the areas of the liberal arts. In the second of these senses the term is sometimes extended to personal cultivation.

Custom. From the Greek con and probably suere ('to make's own'). Thus, a course of action which has become habitual.

Cybernetics. From the Greek kybernetes ('steersman'). The term was introduced by Norbert Wiener and Arturo Rosenblueth for the study of machines in terms of feedback mechanisms.

Cyrenaics. Adherents of a school of philosophy flourishing in the 4th century BC, purportedly founded by Aristippus of Cyrene, bon viveur, and disciple of Socrates. The Cyrenaics maintained that pleasure is the supreme good, identifying 'pleasure' with immediate bodily gratification and denying any positive value to 'mental pleasures' of anticipation and memory or to the cessation of pain. Their grounds were that only our present 'feelings' of pleasure and pain, themselves simply physical motions internal to us, can be truly known to us.

D

Darwin. Charles Robert (1809-82). English biologist. His theory of evolution, set out in the Origin of Species (1859) and The Descent of Man (1871), stated all that kinds of living things developed from, at most, very few simple forms through natural selection among variations

Darshana. Sanskrit term which means 'knowledge' 'vision,' or 'the instrument of vision.' In fact, these meanings coalesce since, in Indian philosophy, an immediate or intuitive vision of reality is the goal of every system. Philosophy and religious practice thus tend to become identical. The term is also used to describe each of the six orthodox systems of philosophy which present themselves as interpretations of the Vedic scriptures.

Darwinism. In the narrow sense the doctrines or organic evolution proposed by Charles Darwin. In the broader sense, those doctrines influenced by Darwin's view.

Dasein. (German for : being there). A term used by Heidegger in the investigation of human existence. Man's particular mode of being-in-the-world is characterized by relatedness to surrounding objects and members of his community, in terms of being concerned with and caring about them. Heidegger distinguishes three constitutive features of Dasein :

1. Faciuality,
2. Existentiality, or the apprehension of his purposive being and potential, and
3. Fallenness, man's tendency to become lost in present preoccupations, forfeiting his unique possibilities and 'authentic' existence.

Datum. From the Latin datus, past participle of dare, 'to give,' hence, the 'given'. Decision concerning what is immediately given provides one of the critical distinctions among philosophies.

Death of God. The 19th-century claim, offered first by Mainlander then by Neitzsche and Sartre, that God is dead. The claim seems an exuberant manner of saying that there is no God and that the belief in God is losing credibility.

Decalogue. The Ten Commandments. The best-known version is to be found in Exodus 20:2-17. A second version is in Deuteronomy 5:6-21. Attributed to Moses, it is more likely that the Decalogue was a product of centuries of deliberation with additions being made even in the 7th century B.C.

Decidable. Denoting a system or theory which is expressed in a logically language where there has been an algorithm for determining, for any correctly formed sentence of the language, whether that sentence is or is not a theorem of that theory. A theorem has been a sentence that is derivable from a theory using rules of logical inference.

Decidability. Refers to one of the basic concepts of contemporary metalogic, along with 'completeness' and 'consistency'. The decidability or undecidability of a formula or sentence in a given system concerns the presence or absence within that system of a method of proof applicable to the formula or sentence, and completable within a finite number of steps.

Deci ion Theory. A relatively new branch of probability theory which is concerned with methods of making optimal decisions in a state of incomplete information, John von Neuman's analysis of game theory.

Decretal. From the Latin decernere ('to decide'). In ecclesiastical history the term referred, initially, to papal decrees as distinguished from the decrees of the Council.

Decurtate Syllogism. From the Latin decurtatus ('curtailed' or 'shortened'). Hence, 'decurtate syllogism' is a synonym for 'enthymeme" a syllogism with a suppressed premise.

Deduction. A vaild argument in which it is impossible to assert the premises and to deny the conclusion without thereby contradicting oneself. The word is not confined within the restrictions of the traditional syllogistic form.

Defeasible. Open to objection. The term is used particularly in connection with concepts, such as legal responsibility, which are presumed to apply unless one or other of a perhaps indeterminate list of defeating conditions obtains. Every person is thus presumed to be legally responsible for what he did: unless the balance of his mind was disturbed; or he could not have known what he was doing or he acted under intolerable duress; or——etc.

Definist Fallacy. One aspect of the naturalistic fallacy: that of confusing two notions by defining one in terms of the other. Moore thought that if 'good' is defined in terms of some natural property, say 'that which produces pleasure', then the open question argument would show that the two were, nevertheless, distinct.

Definite Description. Definite descriptions are important in connection with singular terms, as a singular term without a bearer (or reference) presents problems for the theory of meaning and for logical formalization. For this reason Russell proposed to replace sentences containing definite descriptions by sentences that did not contain them and which, he claimed, were equivalent to the original sentences. In effect, 'The present King of France, is bald' was to be replaced by 'There is something which at present is a King of France and at most one thing at present is a King of France, and that thing is bald'.

Definite Descriptions, Theory of. A theory developed by Russell giving an analysis of descriptive phrases beginning with 'the'.

Definition. Refers to a process or expression that provides the precise meaning of a word or phrase. A definition (definiens), correctly made, will be logically equivalent to the word or phrase being defined (definiendum). Definition may be either of a present established meaning or of a meaning proposed for the future. In the former case the definition is said to be descriptive, in the latter prescriptive or stipulative.

Degrees of Perfection Argument. The fourth of the Five Ways, which contends that, since whatever is the most ϕ must be the cause of whatever else is ϕ, all being and goodness in the Universe must be the work of One who is in these respects The Mostest; 'and this we call God.' Any force that this argument possesses derives from Plato's theory of Forms of Ideas.

De Inesse. Latin phrase from inesse ('being in'). A technical term used by the Schoolmen in two senses :

1. Propositions were said to be de inesse in the simple categorical form where are predicate is affirmed (est in), or denied (non est in) of a subject.

2. Since accidents of substances were held not to exist in their own right (in se), but in something else (in alio), their mode of being with respect to substance was said to be a mode de inesse.

Deism. The doctrine that belief in God can commend itself to the human mind by its own inherent reasonableness, without either being supported by appeals to alleged divine revelations or imposed by religious institutions.

Deism is sometimes seen as exemplifying the vast confidence in reason of the post-Newtonian era.

Demiurge. A term which is derived from the Greek for craftsman :

1. In Plato's Timaeus, the maker of the physical world.

2. The maker acknowledged by most gnostic systems, whose cosmogonic myths depict a demonic being either collaborating with God in creation or seeking to destroy the world by introducing evil.

Democracy. From the Greek demos ('the people') and kratein ('to rule'). Rule by the people may be exercised either directly, as in pure democracy, or through representatives of the people, as in representative democracy.

Democritus of Abdera (c.460—c.370BC). A younger contemporary of Leucippus and a prolific expositor of atomism. He was nicknamed 'the laughing philosopher'. The only fragments of his work that survive are from his ethical writings. These expounded the first rigorously naturalistic (as opposed to supernaturalistic) Greek ethics, and were clearly free to any sophistical amoralism. Democritus was also the subject of the Ph.D. thesis of Marx.

De Morgan's Laws. Laws named after Augustus De Morgan (1806—71), one of the pioneers of the algebraic approach to logic.

(1) is formally stated as $-(p \,\&\, q) \equiv -p \vee -q$; that is to deny a conjunction is to assert the negation of at least one of the conjoined statements (and vice versa);

(2) is formally stated as $-(p \vee q) \equiv -p \,\&\, -q$, that is to deny the disjunction of p and q is to assert both the negation of p and the negation of q (and vice versa).

Denotation. From the Latin de and notare ('to note' or 'mark'). Correlative to the term 'connotation', the denotation of a term is the thing or set of things to which the term refers. The denotation of 'table' is all the tables that exist, have existed, or will exist.

Denying The Antecedent. Q.v. Fallacies (28).

Denying The Consequent. Q.v. Syllogism (10).

Denote. It is sometimes used as equivalent to 'designate', sometimes used to translate Frege's bedeuten and sometimes used to express the relation between a predicate term and everything to which it applies, that is, its extension.

Deontic Logic. Refers to the formulation of logical principles specific to the concept of obligation, such as the impossibility of something being at once both morally obligatory and forbidden.

Deontology. Refers to the ethical theory which is taking duty as the basis of morality; the view that some acts are morally obligatory regardless of their consequences.

Dervish. From the Persian darvish ('beggar'). A member of a Muslim religious order resembling Western monasticism, sometimes mendicant.

Descending Induction. An alternative name for the method of infinite descent.

Descriptions, Theory of. The theory proposed by Russell in order to reveal the underlying logical form of denoting phrases containing descriptions.

Descriptivism. The view that moral judgments have only descriptive, and not presciptive. meaning and can thus be proved by being deduced from statements all straightforwardly factual. Descriptivism is thus a form of ethical naturalism.

Designatum. From the Latin designo ('to mark out or trace'). The referent of a word, symbol, or expression.

Determinism. From the Latin determinare ('to set bounds or limits') The word entered philosophical terminology through Sir William Hamilton who applied the term to Thomas Hobbes in order to distinguish Hobbes' position from fatalism. The position helds that every event or occurrence is 'determined', *i e.,* could not have happened other than it did. The term is opposed to Indeterminism, and to many definitions of free will.

Deus Absconditus. A Latin term which means 'the hidden God'. In contrast to a rationalistic and humanistic approach to theology Luther found the divine hiddeness as much a part of religious experience as the divine presence.

Deus Ex Machina. A Latin phrase which means literally 'a god from a machine'. Referring originally to the maneuver in some classical tragedies of bringing a god on stage to solve the problems of the plot, it refers to anything artificially introduced, as into a philosophy, to solve its inherent difficulties.

Deus Sive Natura. (Latin for; God or Nature.) The phrase used by Spinoza to denote the one infinite 'substance' to which all attributes' must be ascribed.

Deva. A Sanskrit term which means 'bright heavenly one'. Originally designating the nature gods of the Vedic religion, sons of the sky father, Dyaus. Later, the designation for God in Hinduism and Buddhism and of the evil spirits in Zoroastranism. In the latter religion the devas became the daevas or demons, allies of Ahriman, the evil deity in the world struggle between good and evil.

Dhammapada, The. A Sanskrit term which means 'the path of virtue'. The Dhammapada is an early Buddhist document discussing the chief values of life and the path which leads to enlightenment. Moving within the framework of karma and rebirth, the four noble truths of Buddha and eightfold path, the

Dhammapada provides meditations concerning the practice of the way to salvation.

Dharana. The sixth step in Yogic meditation.

Dharma. A Sanskrit term which is having many related meanings. It is the 'law', one of the three jewels of Buddhism. It is custom, justice, religion, culture.

Dhyana. A Sanskrit term which means meditation. Central to the practice of Hinduism. Buddhism, and Jainism, Dhyana forms the seventh stage of yogic meditation, leading to the final stage of Samadhi or 'absorption'.

Diagonal Procedure Refers to the method by which Cantor proved that there are infinite sets that cannot be counted. The real numbers, unlike the rational numbers, are such a non-denumerable set—that is, they cannot be put in a one-to-one correspondence with the natural numbers.

Dialectic

1. (Socratic) The term 'dialectic' is derived from a Greek word that means 'to converse' or 'to discourse', and the dialectic that is ascribed to Socrates is close to this sense.
2. (Platonic) In Plato's Republic, 'dialectic' is the supreme kind of knowledge, which 'gives an account' (logos) of everything—that is, explains everything—by reference to the 'Idea of the Good'.

Dialectical Materialism. Refers to a metaphysical doctrine held by many Marxists. It asserts that matter is primary or fundamental, and states general laws governing the motion and development of all matter. As such, it is distinguished from historical materialism, which is the Marxist theory of history, dealing with the more particular laws governing the development of human society and thought

Dialogue. From the same Greek root as 'dialectic.' meaning 'discourse'.

The term usually refers to the Socratic method of philosophizing through discussion, as set forth in Plato's early dialogues featuring the Socratic figure.

Dianoetic Virtues From the Greek dianoia ('intellect' or 'mind') Thus, the intellectual virtues In Aristotle a distinction is made between intellectual and moral virtues. The former relate to th reasoning function and the apprehension through intellect of rational principles. The latter concern rational control of man's effective nature.

Dichotomy Paradox. The alternative name for the stadium paradox of Zeno of Elea.

Dictum. Latin term which means 'expression' or 'statement'. Used by the Scholastics in relation to modal propositions.

Dictum De Omni Et Nullo. Lattin phrase which means 'principle of everything and nothing.' This is the principle of syllogistic inference as formulated by the Scholastics and grounded in Aristotle. What is predicated universally of a subject or class is predictated of everything falling under the subject or belonging to the class. What is denied universally of a subject or class is denied of everything falling under the subject or belonging to the class.

Difference of Degree. A difference of degree between A and B can be defined in terms of a spectrum of a actual or possible gradations with no apparently natural delineations between them (vagueness). The differences between age and youth, poverty and riches, insanity and sanity—all in human terms of the utmost importance—are of this wrongly despised sort.

Differentia. Refers to that part of the essence of a thing that distinguishes its species from all other species in the same genus.

Dilemma. From the Greek dis ('twice') and lemma ('assumption' or 'premise'). A form of inference of great rhetorical power, the premises consisting of two hypothetical propositions, and one disjunctive proposition and the conclusion being either a disjunctive proposition or a categorical proposition.

Ding An Sich. A German phrase which means 'thing-in-itself.' Introduced by Kant the Ding an sich is the noumenon lying behind reality. The question of the Ding an sich, and especially whether the concept is expendable, assumed importance in neo-Kantianism.

Dionysus. From the Greek dios ('god') and Thracian nusos ('son of' or in some interpretations 'tree'). Thus, alternatively 'tree god' or 'son of god' in literal translation.

Disconfirmation. The opposite of confirmation. It is sometimes called infirmation.

Disjoint. A set-theoretic term describing sets that have no members in common.

Disjunction. From the Latin disjungere ('to disjoin'). In logic, disjunctive propositions are always compound or 'molecular,' and feature the connective 'either-or.' There are strong and weak disjunctions and in traditional logic weak disjunction is termed 'alternation.'

Distributed. Denoting an assertion that is made of all the members of a class. An undistributed assertion is made of less than all the members of a class. 'All Xs are' ϕ is distributed ; Some Xs are ϕ' and This particular X is ϕ' are not.

Distribution. In statistics, the property of a random variable that is identified when a probability is attached to each value of the random variable.

Divine Right of Kings. Derived from the medieval doctrine of the two swords, which latter traced all authority to God, the spiritual sword being granted to the Church and the temporal sword to the state, the divine right of kings held that all authority, spiritual no less than temporal, belongs to the monarch and has been granted him by God. This doctrine of the one sword made its appearance with the rise of the national state.

Division of Powers, Political Doctrine of. Q.v. Montesquieu (7).

Docetism. A Christological doctrine appearing in early Christianity and apparently influenced by Gnosticism, to the effect that the suffering and death of Jesus was only an appearance. These events occurred with respect to a phantom body or shadow.

Docta Ignorantia. Latin phrase which means 'learned ignorance.' a concept employed by Nicholas of Cusa.

Doctrine of the Mean. (Chung Yung in Chinese). The most philosophical of the ancient Chinese documents, the Doctrine of the Mean existed in the ealry Han dynasty.

It is man's goal in life to follow the way. This means achiving equilibrium and harmony. Equilibrium is the state before feelings of pleasure, anger, sorrow, and joy are aroused. Harmony is the state in which they are aroused in due measure and degree.

One's conduct should strike the appropriate mean between deficiency and excess : to serve one's father as one would expect one's son to serve onself ; to serve one's ruler as one expects one's ministers to serve oneself; to serve elder brothers as one expects one's younger brothers to serve oneself; to be the first to treat friends as one would expect to be treated by them. And in all cases one is to do what is proper to his position, and does nht go beyond it.

The three universal virtues are wisdom, humanity, and courage. The five relations they govern are the relations between ruler.

Dogma. A Greek term which 'opinion' or 'decree'.

In substantive form the term has had philosophical use, Dogmatism naming the position of the Fourth Academy, developed by Philo of Larissa.

Dogmatism. The philosophical position of the Fourth Academy.

Double Aspect Theory. In Abbagnano's doctrine of positive existentialism, the theory that every concrete possibility open to man has a positive and a negative aspect.

Double Effect, Principle Of. A principle characteristic of, but not confined to, Roman Catholic moral theology. Where some course of action is likely to have two quite different effects, one licit or mandatory and the other illicit, it may be permissible to take that course intending the one but not the other.

Double Negation. The principle that any proposition implies and is implied by the negation of its negation. Sometimes considered a law of logic, it is the combination of :

(1) the law of non-contradiction (not both p and not-p) and

(2) the law of excluded middle (either p or not-p).

Double Truth, Doctrine Of. The doctrine that what is true in religion may not be true in philosophy, and vice versa.

Doubt. The state of withholding assent from a proposition, and from its contradictory. Moderate doubt is usually known as Skepticism and its extreme form is known as Pyrrhonism.

Doxa. A Greek term which means 'opinion'.

Dualism. A theory concerning the fundamental types into which individual substances are to be divided. It asserts that substances are either material or mental, neither type being reducible to the other.

Duration. From the Latin durare ('to last or endure'). Thus, a stretch of time.

Whatever the genesis of the concept, its philosophical use appears to be related to the contrast of time with eternity. St.

Augustine analyzed the spread of time in psychological terms, finding this concept less clear that of God's eternity, while St. Thomas Aquinas found the term, 'duration', applicable both to time and eternity. Duration and succession apply to time, while eternity is characterized by duration without succession.

Duty. From the Latin debere ('to owe'). The sense of 'duty' vies with that of 'good' or 'value' for the honor of serving as the foundation conception of ethics. Ethical systems taking 'duty' as basic are called 'formalistic' or 'decontological', rather than 'teleological' or 'axiological'.

Dvesa. Sanskrit term signifying the antipathy man develops toward unpleasant things. One of the five kinds of delusive attachment of the Yoga system.

Dyadic. In logic, denoting a predicate or relation, that requires the addition of two singular terms in order to make a well-formed sentence.

Dyaus. From the Sanskrit dyaus ('sky,' 'day').

Dynamism. From the Greek dynamis ('power'). In a general sense any world view asserting the existence of forces in things not reducible to matter in motion.

Dyophysite. One who holds in contrast to Monophysitism the doctrine that two natures, one divine and one human, united in the person of Christ.

Dyothelite. One who holds, in contrast to Monothelitism the doctrine that two wills, one divine and one human, united in the person Christ.

E

Ebionism. The doctrine of the Ebionites, who were the Jewish Christians in Jerusalem, and later merely a sect among them.

Electicism. From the Greek ek ('out') and lego ('select'). An attitude which leads to philosophizing by selection, seeking to bring into harmony what is valid from all philosophers while eliminating the mistaken doctrines of the sources.

Eclecticism. Refers to the principle or practice of taking one's views from a variety of philosophical and other sources.

Ecumenism. A movement, also called the Ecumenical Movement, toward increasing cooperation among the churches and religious orders of the world. Beginning in the West, and still concentrated there, the movement seeks to reverse the Western fragmentation of religious witness.

Eduction. A term now rare, once used to designate immediate inference also used to signify the manner in which the substantial form was drawn from matter in the Aristotelian system.

Education, Philosophy Of. Although an attitude toward education is perhaps implicit in most philosophies, only a small minority have made open declaration of its nature.

Effective Procedure. A procedure (for solving a problem, answering a question, etc) that consists of a finite number of mechanical steps before reaching the answer (to the problem, question, etc.).

Effluxes, Theory Of. The view which was held by the Greek atomists that the surfaces of objects are constantly emitting thin films of atoms (known variously as idola, effluvia, or simulacra) that impinge upon the eye and thus produce the sensation of sight.

EGO. From the Latin ego meaning 'I'. Thus, the individual self.

Egocentric Predicament. In a general sense the problem that we wish to know and interpret the world, and must do so from the perspectives available to us, perspectives centered in ourselves or our egos. In a technical sense the term was introduced by R B. Perry.

Egoism. The doctrine that all of one's actions either are or ought to be self-directed.

Egocentric Particular. Russell's term for a token-reflexive.

Eidetic Images. Mental imagery defined as having the vividness of sense data, but distinguished from hallucinatory sense data as precluding the inclination to believe that there is a genuine perception of a public reality. Eidetic imagery is experienced as projected onto 'the external world'. Those capable of it, usually children, are called eidetikers.

Eidola. A Greek term for 'images'. In the accounts of perception given by Democritus and Epicurus 'detached outlines' given off by objects and received by our senses.

Eidos. (Greek for: form.) The term used by Plato to denote his abstract Forms or Ideas. From it were developed in medieval philosophy the notions of substantial and accidental forms. Objects were to be classified according to their substantial forms, while their accidental forms consisted in any adventitious properties they happened to have had.

Eiufuhlung. A German term which means 'empathy'.

Eleatic. Denoting the philosophy of Parmenides and his followers Zeno of Elea and Melissus of Samos.

Elenchus. In Socratic dialectic, a form of cross-examination that refutes an opponent's thesis by drawing out contradictory or otherwise intolerable consequences from him. Aristotle uses the word to mean 'refutation'.

Elysium Greek term for paradise. Located by Homer on the western edge of the world, by Hesiod and Pindar in the Isles of the Blessed (located in the Western ocean), and, by later poets, in the underworld.

Emanation From the Latin e ('from') and mano ('flow'). Emanation is a doctrine of the overflowing superabundance of the divine. An alternative to the doctrine of creation.

Emanationism. A theory particularly associated with Neoplatonism, which accounts for the source and structure of reality in terms of a perpetual, spontaneous flowing out (emanation) from a transcendent principle, usually called God or the One.

Emergent Evolution. The doctrine that novel qualities, not reducible to their antecedents, appear in the course of evolution. The doctrine was held by C.Lloyd Morgan, Boodin (q.v. 3), Smuts, S. Alexander G.H. Lewes, and others.

Emotivist Theory. The theoey that value terms are grounded in emotional attitudes. Applying initially to the field of ethics, the view has been extended to other areas where values are central, such as aesthetics and social philosophy.

Empathy. This term refers to a state of partial identification with the art object in such fashion that one's relation to the object combines the senses of both identity and distance.

Empiricism. Usually defined as the thesis that all knowledge or at least all knowledge of matters of fact as distinct from that of purely logical relations between concepts—is based on experience.

Empiriocriticism. Refers to an empirical, positivist approach to epistemology which was developed by Richard Avenarius and criticized by Lenin in Materialism and Empirio-Critism (1909).

Empty Set. The null set.

Enantiomorphs. A pair of objects related to each other as a right hand is to a left, or as opposite spirals are, or mirror images. Kant, in Prolegomena used them in an argument in favour of the concept of absolute (as opposed to relative) space.

Encyclopedists. In philosophy the term is usually reserved for the group of 18th-century French philosophers, known as les philosophes who, motivated by the view that social evils could be eliminated throgh the spread of knowledge, collaborated in the project of composing the thirty-five volume French Encyclopedie (1751-80) designed to bring all knowledge into a single compass. Editor of the encyclopedia was Denis Diderot who wrote most of the articles on religion, ancient history, and political theory.

Fnergeia. A Greek term which means 'energy', 'action', or 'operation'. As utilized by Aristotle the term signifies both a state of realized potentiality and the activity leading to that state. In both senses the term stands in marked contrast to dynamis ('unrealized potentiality').

Enligbtenment (or Age of Reason). The era characterized by the emergence, in 18th-century France, of progressive and liberal ideas that led to the Revolution and remained influential in western philosophy. Increasing scientific knowledge gave rise to the development of empiricist, naturalist, and materialist doctrines and strong opposition to clericalism. It was the era that saw the publication of the Encyclopedie.

Ens Realissimum. (Latin for ; the most real being.) God, the absolute possessor of all realities and all the attributes of perfection. The term is used In Kants, discussion of proofs of God's existence.

Entelechy

(1) For Aristotle the entelechy of a thing is both its complete reality and the power of the developing thing to achieve completeness or perfection. Also, q.v. Energeia.

(2) Leibniz applied the term to the monads of his system, apparently because they possess both of the qualities mentioned in (1) above.

Enthymeme

1. A syllogism having a suppressed premise.

2. A conditional holding on formally-reducible material grounds.

Entity. From the Laitn ens, entis ('thing'). In Scholastic philosophy, initially, any real being. Later, whatever has sufficient separateness of being, whether in reality or thought, to support preci-cations.

Enumeration. The term has at least two philosophical connections.

(1) One of the forms of definition is 'definition by emumeration.' This is a definition by listing the individuals or sub-classes making up the denotation of the term.

(2) One of the forms of induction is 'induction by simple enumeration' (also called perfect or complete induction). The form was criticized by Francis Bacon who argued for the 'experimental method.'

Epagoge. From the Greek meaning 'a bringing in.' A Greek and Aristotelian term for induction Instances of induction are sometimes called 'epagogic demonstrations' or 'epagogic syllogisms.'

Epicureanism. The philosophy of Epicurus and his followers, combining an ethical hedonism with a theory that all things are really atoms and void. Reformulating these doctrines in such a way as to counter various points in Plato and Aristotle, Epicurus built them into a recognizably Hellenistic system, with ethics supported by physics and epistemology.

Epicureanism. A school of philosophy founded in Athens in 306 B.C. by Epicurus (q.v.). The school, stressing atomic theory, empiricism, and hedonism, remained an influential factor in the cultural life of Greece and Rome from the time of Epicurus in the 4th century B.C. until the 5th century A D. During this period there is a long record of the polemic between the Epicureans on the one hand and the Stoics, Skeptics and the Aristotelian or Peripatetic philosophers on the other.

Epiphenomenalism. A doctrine concerned with the relationship between mind and body, advanced in the late 19th century as an alternative to the theories of interaction and parallelism.

Epiphenomenon. A secondary or added accompaniment to a process, considered as merely incidental and having no part in the further development of the process.

Epistemics. A term coined in Edinburgh University in 1969 to label a new school dedicated to the scientific, as opposed to the philosophical, study of knowledge.

Epistemology. The branch of philosophy which is concerned with the theory of knowledge. Traditionally, central issues in epistemology are the nature and derivation of knowledge, the scope of knowledge, and the reliability of claims to knowledge.

Episyllogism. A syllogism one or both of whose premises forms the conclusion of a preceding syllogism.

Epoche. A Greek term for "suspense of judgment."

(1) The term was used both by Skeptics and members of the Academy as the appropriate response to the problem of knowledge. 'Suspense of judgment' was regarded as leading to ataraxia, or pleasure in tranquility.

(2) Husserl has adopted the term, insisting upon epoche, or suspense of judgment, as a stage in the phenomenological reduction.

'E' Proposition. Q.v. Proposition (1); Syllogism (3; 6b).

Equality. Most analyses of the human condition do not find men equal, although the claim in the natural rights doctrine is that all have equal rights Rousseau held equality to be 'unnatural'.

Equivalence Relation. Any transitive, symmetric, and reflexive relation Whenever two things a and b are equivalent, or identical in some respect P, the relation expressed by 'x is the same as y in respect of P' will be an equivalence relation. For example, two rods, of whatever material, may or may not have the same length. For some purposes all rods of the same length are equivalent and the relation given by 'x is the same as y in respect of length' is an equivalence relation over the class of rods.

Equivalent

1. (material) Two statements are said to be materially equivalent when they have the same truth-value.

2. (formal) Two statements A and B are said to be formally equivalent when A may be deduced from B alone by valid argument, and vice versa.

3. (logical) Two statements A and B are said to be logically equivalent when it is impossible that they should have different truth-values.

Equivoeal. Having two meanings.

Equivocate. To employ equivocal words or expressions, confounding their meanings.

Equivocation. From the Latin aeques ("equal") and vocare "(to call"). The sense is that of regarding a word used in two senses as carrying the same meaning when, in fact, the meaning differ.

Erastianism. The term used for the belief that secular authority should have supremacy over the Church in all matters.

Eristic. From the Greek eris ('strife'). In Aristotle a mode of argument having as its goal victory in disputation, and thus to be distinguished both from science and from dialectic. The Megarian School of Philosophy is associated with eristic.

Erotetic. Concerning questions, interrogatory. The term is used especially in connection with the logical analysis of questions (also called erotetic logic).

Error. Originally, a Latin term meaning "a wandering about." Since to fall into error means that one has missed the truth what is said under the latter entry applies here as well. How one falls into error has been the subject of philosophical discussion.

Esoterism. From the Greek esoteros ('inner,' 'interior'). The doctride that ancient wisdom contains an esoteric part, separate from public writings or lectures available to all (the exoteric part).

Esse. (Latin for : to be.) A term used in scholastic philosophy for existence.

Esse Est Percipi. Latin phrase meaning 'To be is to be perceived.' A slogan of Berkeley the statement has had importance for other philosophers as well.

Essence. The notion of a fixed and timeless possibility of existence, derived from Aristotle by his medieval interpreters. Aristotle had taught that the definition of a thing expressed the thing's essence, the characteristics it had to have to be the thing it was.

Essentialism. A term which designates three separate philosophical positions :

1. The doctrine, in Plato, of the existence of Forms, that is, of really existing abstract entities of which physical objects are imperfect copies.

2. A position holding that something can have an essential property in virtue of a definition, or as described in a certain way.

3. Perhaps the most important, a metaphysical view dating back to Aristotle, certain aspects of which are currently much discussed. It maintains that some objects—no matter how described—have essences; that is, they have, essentially or necessarily, certain properties, without which they could not exist or be the things they are. This is often seen as equivalent to the claim that there are de re modalities.

Eternal

1. Everlasting.

2. Non-temporal. Plato's Forms or Ideas should surely be thought of as the latter rather than the former; and, if so, his attempt in Phaedo to base a doctrine of the temporal immortality of the soul upon that theory must have been misconceived.

Eternal Recurrence. A doctrine, holding that time is cyclical, to be found in both East and West: in Hinduism in Greek philosophy in some medieval thinkers and in modern philosophy.

Eternity. From the Latin aeternus (from aeviternus, in turn from aevum, 'age'). The problem of time and eternity turns, at least in part, on the ideas of permanence and change. Time is the order of change and eternity is the order of changelessness.

Ethical Intuitionism. The view that ethical terms are primary and underived, *i.e* , different in nature from all non-ethical terms and thereby not wholly definable.

Ethical Naturalism. The view that ethics is a part of the natural world, and that ethical issues can be settled by an appeal to facts.

Ethics As a philosophical term 'ethics' has clear connections, though it is not identical, with this everyday usage. Like all philosophical endeavour it is an investigation into the fundamental principles and basic concepts that are or ought to be found in a given field of human thought and activity. Being a branch of philosophy it is a theoretical study. As such it differs from 'ethics' in the lay sense outlined above, in that any actual body of ethical belief, for example, Christian ethics, will be intended to be a practical guide to living and not merely an exposition and analysis of certain theoretical doctrines.

Etiology. From the Greek aitia ('cause') and logos ('theory of'). Thus, the study of causality, usually as restricted to a given class of phenomena.

Eudaemonism From the Greek eudaimonia ('happines'). The term refers literally to the condition of being blessed by the protection of a benign spirit. Applied to all ethical theories taking happiness as man's chief end, the term is attributed primarily, and most commonly, to the ethics formulated by Aristotle

Euhemerism. The view that the gods originated from popular heroes.

Eulogon. The doctrine of Arcesilas that probability is the guide to life.

Eurytus of Croton. A follower of Pythagoras, known only for his procedure as associating particular creatures with, and representing them by, particular numbers of pebbles. The most plausible interpretation of this practice is that he considered that the essence of a sort of objects consists in the points required to bound the surfaces of those objects.

Euthanasia. In its etymological origins 'good dying', but currently confined to an easy death as an escape from some condition, usually terminal, and felt by the patient to be intolerable.

Eutychianism. The Christological doctrine that at the incarnation Christ's human nature was absorbed into the divine nature. The doctrine was introduced by Eutychus, head of a monastery outside Constantinople, between 448 and 451 A.D. Since Eutychianism denied that Christ had two distinct natures, and implied that God Himself was tempted, suffered, and died, the doctrine was condemned and Eutychus was excommunicated.

Evaluative. Tending to concern or suggest rules or standards, as opposed to purely descriptive. An evaluative statement implies a value judgement on the part of the person making it.

Event. An occurrence (as opposed to a material object), usually thought of as happening at a determinable time nnd place.

Evidence. That which proves or contributes to the proof of a conclusion. The problem of evidence involves the question of the criterion for truth.

Evil. From Anglo-Saxon yfel. The opposite and complement of good, the term is almost always defined negatively. Evil has been treated from both religious and philosophical points of view.

Evolution. From the Latin e ('out') and volvere ('to roll'). The idea of evolution is, in a general sense, a subdivision of the problem of the one and the many, or the problem of permanence and change. If the concept of evolutionary development is taken with sufficient generality it can be shown to have characterized philosophical thought from the beginning, and almost continuously.

Excluded Middle, Principle of. One of the three laws of thought. The principle holds that, as Aristotle said, there is nothing between the two parts of a contradiction. Either the proposition p is true, or the contradictory of p is true.

Exemplarism. From the Latin exemplum ('model' or 'example'). The term refers to the Platonic-inspired doctrine that finite things are copies of divine ideas. The phrase, exemplary cause, similarly, refers to the causal role of exemplars.

Existence. From the Latin ex and sistere ('to step forth, emerge'). Philosophical analyses of the concept of existence are in some respects similar to analyses of the concept of matter. As 'matter' stands in contrast to 'form,' so 'existence' stands in contrast to 'essence.' And since mental activity is concerned with the characteristics of things the latter terms, 'form' and 'essence,' seem less puzzling than 'matter' and 'existence.' If 'existence' cannot be characterized, how is one to discuss it; and if it can be characterized how does it stand in contrast to 'essence'? The puzzle is not far removed from the following analyses.

Existentialism. A philosophical movement challenging essentialism and concentrating attention on the human situation. Theistic existentialism is usually regarded as beginning with Kierkegaard and atheistic, existentialism with Nietzsche.

Existential Quantifier. The notation used in Existential Ge eralization and Instantiation.

Experience. From the Latin experior ('to prove' or 'to put to the test'). The usual use of the term is to refer to information gained from the senses rather than from reason.

Explanation. From the Latin ex and planare ('to make level or plain'). The procedure of making a matter clear consists of dividing a complex idea into its simpler parts, or in demonstrating that the idea in question can be deduced from certain premises, or that a state of affairs would have resulted from certain causes, or in a combination of these procedures. That which is to be explained is called the explanandum; that which provides the explanation is called the explanans.

Explication

1. In general, explanation.
2. (in logic) A form of analysis by which an imprecise concept is given a precise formal definition in order to make it suitable for formal logical use.

Extension. That which has spatial dimentions. The concept was used by Descartes to distinguish matter, which is extended or has extension, from mind, which he regarded as a thinking substance having no spatial dimensions.

External Relation. A relation independent of its terms. The discussion of external relation was of importance in the late 19th and early 20th centuries.

External World. The philosophical problem set by Descartes when, in his 'room with a stove', he argued that his only rock bottom certainty was his immediate present consciousness : 'I think, therefore I am.' The problem was to show whether, starting from there, anyone could know, and how he could know, that there was a universe around him, containing things and other people. It should be remembered that the Cartesian starting point is a subject of consciousness both solitary and incorporeal.

Extrasensory Perception (or ESP). The various putative phenomena of acquiring information without any employment of the senses.

Extrinsic Value. Correlate of intrinsic value. The phrase applies to things or states of being valuable not in themselves but in their consequences. 'Instrumental value' is a synonym.

F

Fa Chia. A Chinese term meaning 'legalist school.' One of the ancient Chinese schools of philosophy.

Fact/Value Distinction. The argument against rationalistic ethics, first advanced by Hume, claiming that reason alone cannot grasp or be the grounds for moral approval or disapproval.

Faculty Psychology. From the Latin facere ('to make'). A view of psychology in which mind, psyche, or soul is analyzed into the separate faculties, or powers, of reason, will and sensibility.

Faith. From the Latin fidere ('to trust'). An attitude of belief which goes beyond the available evidence. There are both religious and non-religious forms of faith.

Religious faith enters philosophy as a significant problem, especially in relation to the claims of inquiry. The problem of faith and reason has had a long and continuing history.

Fallacies. From the Latin fallacia ('deceit,' 'trick,' or 'fraud'). The problem of validity in logic has its other side in the recognition of types of invalidity. Since fallacies are instances of reasoning which violate the requirements of validity, and since there exists an indefinitely great number of possible ways of reasoning improperly, there can be no conprehensive list of fallacies.

Fallacy. An argument involving an invalid, rather than a valid, form of reasoning.

Fallibilism. A theory presented by Peirce describing enquiry as an activity generated by a state of unease and aiming to attain a state of rest through finding the right answer to a question. But rest is never assured, since no one can know what fresh evidence might present itself to necessitate a change in position.

Falsidical. Saying what is false ; a word created by philosophers as an opposite for veridical.

Falsification. Showing or demonstrating to be false. In this philosophical sense, as opposed to its ordinary, non-technical sense of 'making false by alteration or deception', this word refers to the precise opposite of verification.

Fascism. From the Latin fascis, the bundle of rods—including an ax with blade projecting—carried as a symbol of authority before the magistrates of Rome. The name of an Italian political organization founded by Mussolini in 1919, bringing him to power in 1922. Gentile and Ugo Spirito contributed to the theory of the corporate state which Fascists held to be their goal.

Fatalism. The doctrine that all things happen according to an inexorable fate. The doctrine is both pre-philosophical and pre-theological. The equivalent doctrine in theological thought is pre-destination, and in philosophy its equivalent is determinism.

Fatalism. Refers to the doctrine that what will happen will happen, and nothing we do or do not do will make any difference. It can of course be held either about everything and everyone or in more restricted forms.

Fate. From the Latin fatum (the Greek term is moira), both terms meaning 'a prophetic declaration or oracle.' The fated is that which is destined or decreed to come to pass. The term is pre-philosophical, deriving from mythology. In Arabic the term is kismet; it means 'fate,' 'destiny,' 'the will of Allah.

Feeling. Any portion of one's awareness characterized by sensation or emotion.

Fictionalism. For Hans Vaihinger the doctrine that fictitious entities, useful but imaginary concepts and principles, lie at the basis of mathematics, science, philosophy, law, and religion.

Fideism. The view, recurrent throughout religious history, that essential religious doctrines cannot be established by rational means, but only accepted, if at all, by acts of faith. Its extreme form holds that religion requires the acceptance of doctrines actually absurd or contrary to reason (quia impossible).

Fides Quaerens Intellectum. (Latin for : faith seeking understanding.) A slogan coined by St. Augustine to characterize the Christian intellectual quest.

Figure. In logic, one of the four possible arrangements of the terms in a categorical syllogism. Aristotle distinguished only three figures; the isolation of the fourth is traditionally attributed to Galen. Syllogism.

Figure, Galenian. The fourth figure of the syllogism named after Galen who added it to the three figures of Aristotle.

Final Cause. That one of Aristotle's four causes which supports the hylozoistic interpretation of matter. Final cause has human purposiveness as its paradigm, and generalizes purpose beyond the human realm. One must suppose, with Aristotle, that the unttained state of the oak can exercise causal power over the acorn.

Finite Set. Refers to a set that is either empty, or is such that there exists a one-to-one correspondence between its members and a subset of the set of natural numbers less than a specified natural number.

Finitism. Refers to an approach to mathematics that admits to the domain of mathematics only objects (numbers) that are capable of construction in a finite number of steps.

First Cause. One of the names of God, derived from the argument—formulated by Aristotle—that every causal chain requires a first, uncaused cause.

First Heaven. For Aristotle, the outermost sphere, identified with the region of the fixed stars.

First Mover. The origin of all motion in the Universe, an origin that is itself unmoved. The idea was introduced by Aristotle and developed by philosopher-theologians in all the three great traditions of Mosaic theism—Judaism, 'Christianity and Islam'.

First Philosophy. In Aristotle's sense the study of being as being. This, along with Theology, is the name Aristotle gave to the book we now call Metaphysics, and to the discipline as well, a study of the concepts existing within and extending beyond specific fields of inquiry.

Flatus Vocis. Latin phrase meaning 'mere word'. Anselm and Abelard charged that Roscelin held the universal to be a mere word, thus opening the issue of nominalism with respect to the problem of universals.

Flying Arrow Paradox. The arrow paradox of Zeno of Elea.

Force. From the Latin fortis ('strong'). In physics the cause of the acceleration in the movement of material bodies. As the etymology of the word suggests, the conception had its origin in human effort, and was transferred to the physical world.

Aristotle making locomotion the primary motion, was led to interpret force in mechanical terms, requiring contact between bodies. In his view there is a direct proportional relation between force, time, and distance. The view was immensely influential, and only gradually were other alternatives suggested.

Foreknowledge. The doctrine that God has knowledge of the future by virtue of His eternity, all events being present to Him in totum simul. It is sometimes argued that in this manner the divine Omniscience is compatible with human freedom.

Form. From the Latin forma (probably from ferire 'to strike, hew', thus to create a recognizable thing). Forma is a translation of the Greek term idea or eidos.

For Plato the individual thing with its class character is explained by the interaction of form and receptacle. The form is received in matter. This constitutes the individual thing and makes it an imitation of the eternal form in which it participates. In this view the eternal forms possess a higher reality than do their temporal imitations.

Formal Cause. Aristotle (9); Form (5f).

Formal Distinction. Duns Scotus (6).

Formalism. The tendency to emphasize form as over against content. In ethics the tendency is most pronounced in Kant and in Deontological Ethics generally.

Formal Language. An uninterpreted system of signs. The signs are typically of three sorts :

(1) variables, for example, sentence letters p, q, r, s;

(2) connectives, for example, $\vee$, &, $\rightarrow$, by which signs are joined together; and

(3) punctuation devices, such as brackets, to remove ambiguity.

Formally and Eminently. Scholastic technical terms still used without explanation by Descarts. Thus Meditation VI argues that the power producing what would now be called sense data 'resides in some substance different from me, in which all the reality subjectively in the ideas produced is formally or eminently contained.' The second term means in a pre-eminent manner or degree, the first specifies a straightforward correspondence with what is found in the effect. Descartes here appeals to that supposed a priori knowledge of causality which Hume was later to deny.

Formal Mode of Speech. Refers to the employment of all the various devices for making it unequivocally clear that the true subject of discourse is, where it is, concepts and the logical relations between concepts, rather than objects or events and the supposed contingent facts about those objects or events. The contrast is with material mode of speech. Both expressions were introduced by Rudolf Carnap.

Formal System (or Theory). Refers to any set of axioms and/or rules of inference written in some specified formal language L. The axioms will be closed wffs (wff) of L, and rules of inference (or transformation rules) are rules according to which proofs can be constructed out of wffs of L.

Formation Rules. Rules defining, often inductively, the notion of a wff (well-formed formula) of a language.

Four Elements, The. Earth, air, fire and water were regarded as the basic constituents of the universe in many ancient cosmologies.

Four Humours. The four body fluids that Galen believed must be held in equilibrium to maintain mental and physical well-being. They were blood, choler (yellow bile), phlegm, and melancholy (black bile). The doctrine, like that of the four elements, survived until the 17th century, forming the basis of medieval physiology and clinical medicine.

Four-term Fallacy. Refers to a form of defective syllogism that is deficient because the middle term occurs in two distinct senses. Thus 'All kinds cry. That goat is a kid. Therefore that goat cries'.

Frankfurt School. A movement associated with the Institute for Social Research founded within the University of Frankfurt in 1923. It has included Max Horkheimer, Theodor Adorno and Herbert Marcuse. The uniting idea is the need for a critical Marxism, construed as involving rejection of positivism, value-freedom, and (crude) materialism, while stressing the actual Hegelian and alleged idealist side of Marx himself.

Fravashi. Guardian angles of the faithful in Zoroastrianism.

Freedom. From the Middle English fredom ('the state of being free'). The quality of not being constrained by fate, necessity, or circumstance in one's decisions and actions.

Freewill and Determinism. Two apparently opposed philosophical concepts: the former postulating that man is able to choose and act according to the dictates of his own will, the latter that all events including human actions, are predetermined. Perplexities arise for both the secularist and still more the theist.

Function. One of the most central concepts in mathematics. It comes to have application in logic as a result of Frege's insistence (in 'Function and Concept') on the analogy between concepts and functions. However, with the increasing use of formal logic in the study of the foundations of mathematics, functions themselves have become objects of study in logic itself.

Function. From the Latin functio from fungi ('to perform, execute'). In symbolic logic, an expression involving one or more variable terms whose meaning or truth is determined when the values of the variables are specified.

Future. Along with past and present, one of the three divisions of time. Determinists generally hold that the future is closed, although not yet occurrent; indeterminists hold that it is open.

G

Galenian Figure. The fourth figure of the syllogism.

Galileo Galilei (1564-1642). Italian mathematician, astronomer, and physicist who founded modern mechanics and cogently argued for the Copernican heliocentric theory of the universe. His views brought him into constant conflict with the religious authorities. In 1633 he was forced to recant and was placed under house arrest for the remainder of his life.

Gallicanism. The movement leading to the Gallican Articles.

Gambler's Fallacy. The belief into which a gambler may be tempted, to the effect that a system such as a roulette wheel or a tossed coin has a 'memory', so that after a run of one kind of result another outcome becomes more probable. The fallacy lies in supposing that the so-called law of averages implies this. In fact the theorem applies only where probabilities are constant from repetition to repetition, and so can offer no support to the gambler's belief.

Game Theory. A mathematical theory dealing with game-like situations in which participants wish to maximize some property (such as utility) in positions of uncertainty, not only with respect to the state of nature but also the actions of other players whose interests may be opposed or parallel to those of the participant.

Gandhi, Mohandas K. (1869-1948). Indian religious and national leader. Born in Porbandar. Educated in London. Called Mahatma ('great soul'), he combined Hindu, Christian, and philosophic principles in a version of pacifism which included the idea of 'passive resistance'. Thoreau and Tolstoy are specifically credited as having contributed to his thinking.

Gathas. The hymns ascribed to Zoroaster in the Avesta, sacred scriptures of Zoroastrianism.

Gaudapada. 6th or 8th Century A.D. Indian philosopher. The first known systematic exponent of Advaita Vedanta the non-dualistic interpretation of the Vedanta philosophy. Influenced by Nagarjuna and Vasubandhu, Gaudapada's basic attachment was to the Upanishads. Indeed, one thrust of his work lies in showing that both Buddhism and Vedanta are rooted in the Upanishadic literature.

Gemara. An Aramaic term meaning 'completion'. A body of literature amplifying the Mishnah.

Generative Grammar. The rules that allow speakers to construct (generate) infinite numbers of new sentences in a language.

Generation. From the Latin generare ('to beget, create'). One of the Aristotelian types of change. Its opposite is 'corruption'. Generation is a change from non-being to being, while corruption is a change from being to non-being. Relative generation and corruption are types of alteration or change of quality, regarded by Aristotle as one of the three basic types of change. Absolute generation and corruption, although recognized by Aristotle, remain something of a mystery within his system.

Genetic. From the Greek genesis ('origin').

(1) As an adjective the term applies to an investigation into origins.

(2) The Genetic Fallacy is committed when the latter stages of a process are evaluated only in terms of its earlier stages.

Genetic Fallacy. The mistake of arguing that because something is now such and such, therefore it must already have been such and such at an earlier stage; or, because it was such and such then, therefore it must be the same now.

Genus In Aristotelian logic, a very wide and comprehensive class or kind, sub-classes of which may be called species. Generally in philosophy neither term carries its peculiar biological implications.

Geometry. A science that has its origins practically located in the need of the ancient Egyptians to redraw field boundaries each year as a result of the Nile floods; the laws concerning lines, angles, etc., being arrived at by empirical generalization. The Greeks, in particular Euclid (c. 300 BC), turned geometry into a deductive theoretical science based on certain postulates, which in recent times has been rigorously axiomatized using only the primitive terms 'point', 'between', and 'congruent'.

Gestalt. A German term meaning 'form, shape, or figure.' The term stands for the principle that perceptual content is a series of configurations or totalities, rather than a series of simple perceptual elements.

Ghost in the Machine. A label introduced by Gilbert Ryle in The Concept of Mind (1949) to describe a thesis of Descartes to the effect that, while the human body may be regarded as an enormously subtle and complicated machine, it only becomes a person when it is joined by an incorporeal soul.

Gilgamesh Epic. A work of Assyrian Babylonian literature going back to Sumerian legends 3000 years before Christ. The narrative of the wanderings of Gilgamesh and his friend, Engidu (half-man=half-bull), contains an account of a flood, called the Babylonian Flood Story, of which the Biblical account is a variant.

Given, The. An obsolete term for the putative raw data of experience—uncontaminated by theoretical, ordering, or inferential impositions or additions.

Gnoseology. An obsolete synonym for epistemology.

Gnosticism. From the Greek gignoskein meaning 'to know.' Gnosticism is not, as the name implies, a movement committed to the increase of genuine knowledge, but a philosophic-religious movement related to the mystery religions and directed toward personal salvation Gnosticism, like the mystery religions, claimed an esoteric wisdom, sharply distinguishing between the uninitiated and the initiated.

God. An Anglo-Saxon term of Teutonic origin referring to the object of religious worship. Its meaning, therefore, is as varied as human culture itself. The concept has developed in different ways in different settings. A great deal of evidence supports the view that the origin of the conception lies in the numinous feeling linking primitive man to his world, and issuing in animism, mana, and sympathetic magic. It is tempting to say, although arranging cultural stages is hazardous, that the end of this development, given polytheism as an intermediate stage, is monotheism.

Godel's Theorem. The proof, published by Kurt Godel in 1931, of the existence of formally undecidable propositions in any formal system of arithmetic. More precisely, his first incompleteness theorem (which is what is usually meant when people talk of Godel's theorem) states that in any formal system S of arithmetic, there will be a sentence P of the language of S such that if S is consistent, neither P nor its negation can be proved in S. The technique used in proving this result is to translate the syntax of the language of S into arithmetic, thus making S capable of representing its own syntax. This makes it possible to show that there must be a sentence P of S which can be interpreted (very roughly) as saying 'I am not provable.

God of the Gaps. The hostile phrase applied to theories appealing to the concept of God to explain anything science currently finds inexplicable, for instance, the origins of life or of consciousness. Theologians now generally regard such appeals as creating only the illusion of explanation, and providing no valid basis or support for theism.

Golden Age. In Greek mythology, a time of paradisal innocence under the rule of Cronus, son of Uranus (Heaven) and Gaea (Earth). The idea of the golden age became a potent literary and artistic emblem for a perfect and harmonious relationship between man and Nature and between man and man.

Golden Mean. Moderation in a person's course of life. Aristotle saw the mean as the rational and virtuous course between extremes of excess—for example, temperance shunning both asceticism and profligacy.

Golden Rule. Stated negatively by Confucious 'What you do not want done to yourself, do not do to others,' and positively by Jesus 'Do unto others, as you would have others do unto you,' the rule is widely held to be the basis of all morality.

Good. From Anglo-Saxon god Latin bonum, and Greek agathon. The idea of the good, or of value, plays a role in all philosophical areas but primarily in Ethics, Aesthetics, and Axiology.

The distinction between instrumental and intrinsic goodness, or value, begins with the Greeks. Intrinsic goods are those things good in themselves; instrumental goods have their value in making possible another good.

Goodman's Paradox. A linguistic paradox of confirmation or prediction. We predict by projecting regularities beyond our experience (induction). Goodman showed how to define a vocabulary so that hypotheses that look to us as though they predict change have the linguistic from of projecting a regularity Goodman introduces a new predicate 'grue', which applies to an object if it has been examined before a certain time t and is green, or has not been examined before t and is blue.

Grace. The term entered theology obliquely by way of the three graces, fate fortune, and providence. In theology, grace is the favor, relating to salvation, shown to man by God.

Grammatical Form. The apparent surface form of an expression, in comparison with the underlying logical structure.

Granth. The sacred book of the Sikhs (Sikhism).

Greatest Happiness Principle (or Principle of Utility). The basic tenet of utilitarianism, which holds that the supreme good is the greatest happiness of the greatest number of people. Happiness is construed as the maximization of pleasure and minimization of pain; it is contended that only in terms of this programme do concepts like 'good', 'duty', and 'right' have meaning and application.

Greek Philosophy. The period of Greek philosophy can be said to run from around 600 B.C. to 600 A.D In this period of greater than a thousand years not only were all the philosophical alternatives of the Western world sketched out, but many of the scientific theories which have gained acceptance since that time: among these are the atomic theory, the heliocentric view of the solar system, and organic evolution. The philosophical alternatives occur usually in schools of philosophy.

Grelling's Paradox (or Paradox of Heterologicality). A semantic paradox presented by K. Grelling (1886—) in 1908. Some words have the same property as that which they name: for example, 'short' is a short word and 'polysyllabic' has many syllables. These words are called 'homological' (or 'autological'). In contrast, heterological words such as 'useless' or monosyllabic' are not instances of the properties they name. The paradox arises when considering the word 'heterological' itself: if it is heterological, then it does not instantiate it meaning—but this is what 'heterological' means, therefore the word is homological. Conversely, if 'heterological' is autological, then in must have the characteristic of applying to itself and therefore 'heterological' is heterological.

Guelfs. A term in use in the 13th and 14th century to signify those who favored the spiritual power in contrast with the Ghibellines who favored temporal power. The terms were used throughout Italy and Germany, referring to the struggles between papacy and feudal nobility, and the emerging urban classes against the feudallords.

H

Habit. From the Latin habitus ('state or appearance') from habere ('to have, be in a condition'). The Greek term lexis is Aristotle's term for this state or condition of body or mind.

Aristotle utilized the concept of habit in his ethics to explain how a disposition to act virtuously is developed from the more capacity to so act. The disposition to act virtuously results from virtuous habits, and the habit is built upon virtuous activity. The circularity seems not to be vicious. Thomas Aquinas follows Aristotle here.

Haecceity. From the Latin haecceitas which means 'thisness' or 'specificity.' The principle of individuation of Duns Scotus. Approximations to the view are to be found also in other Schoolmen, especially those of the Oxford school. 'Thisness' is presented as an alternate to matter as the means of understanding the step from infima species (the smallest species) to individual thing.

Halakha. A Hebrew term which means 'practice' or 'rule.'

Happiness. From middle English hap, old Norse happ meaning 'good luck.' Also in Greek eudaimonia means 'to be prosperous or well-off' as well as 'to be happy'.

In fulfillment theories of valuation, happiness, as a state of being somehow different from a sum of pleasures, stands as the end of life. Aristotle's view of happiness sets the pattern in this respect. Epicurus defined happiness, largely at least, in terms of pleasure with prudence an important ancillary value. Aquinas followed Aristotle although adding a theological dimension.

Harmony. From the Greek harmos ('a fitting or joining'). The principle has played a role, modest but continuing, in the philosophy both of the East and of the West.

In the ancient Chinese Doctrine of the Mean the term is defined as a state in which the feelings of pleasure, anger, sorrow and joy are aroused in 'due measure and degree,' and contrasted with 'equilibrium,' the state prior to the arousal of such feelings.

Hasidism. A pietistic mass movement that began among Jews in early 18th century Russia. Its philosophical roots were in the Kabbalah.

Hatha-yoga. The term used for the Indian system of mental and physical training, which has been based on certain speculative physiological theories and is intended to give an individual control over his own physical and spiritual well-being. It is commonly known in the West as yoga, but is not to be confused with the Yoga school of philosophy, with which it shares certain techniques of meditation.

Hedonism

1. (in ethics) The principle that happiness (defined in terms of pleasure) is the sole and proper aims of human action.

2. (in psychology) The doctrine that no one in fact ever does or ever can act save to further his own pleasure.

Hegelianism. The views of those who claim to uphold the doctrines of Hegel have shown considerable differences, not only because of the obscurity of Hegel's writings, but also because there was a fundamental ambivalence in his views. Hegel had argued that history is a process which has a rational end, and soon after his death there was disagreement among his followers about the rationality of the state that history had reached. The so called Old Hegelians argued that contemporary political conditions were rational; the Young Hegelians disagreed, and said that the business of philosophy was to promote a revolution—more specifically, a revolution of ideas.

Heidelberg School. One of the schools of neo-Kantian philosophy active during the last part of the 19th and the first part of the 20th century. Located at the University of Heidelberg, the school took an axiological approach to Kant, holding value to be the key to epistemology.

Heilsgeschichte. A German term which means 'holy history' or the 'history of holiness.' A Protestant view of history, arising under this name in the 18th century, which held that the purpose of history is the gradual formation of the Chosen People under the guidance of the Holy Spirit.

Heliocentric Theory. The theory, first advanced by Aristarchus of Samos (310-230 BC) that the earth and planets revolve round the sun, which remains fixed, and that the earth rotates on its own axis throughout its orbit. Revived by Copernicus in refuting the Ptolemaic system, and upheld by Galileo, the idea of the earth not being at the centre of the universe was opposed as much in the times of Aristarchus as in 16th and 17th-century Europe, on the grounds that it depreciated man's place in the Universe.

Hellenistic Philosophy. The Hellenistic period in Greek history runs from 323 BC, the year of Alexander the Great's death, to 30 BC when the last major Hellenistic empire was annexed by Rome. Philosophy in this period centred on Athens. Of the four major schools there (Academic, Peripatetic, Epicurean, and Stoic), the Epicureans, with their hedonistic ethics and (denial of providence, were the outsiders. The contrary belief derived ultimately from Socrates) in a purposive universe and in the right exercise of reason as the supreme human good found its most forceful advocates in the Stoics. Their principal opponents came from the Academy of Athens with its 'sceptical' rejection of all positive 'dogmatic' belief. Controversy between Stoics and Academics dominated the philosophical scene in the 3rd and 2nd centuries BC. Later there arose a tendency, variously represented by Panaetius, Posidonius, and Antiochus, to combine Stoicism with the Platonic and Aristotelian doctrines, that ultimately submerged it.

Henological Argument. Refers te an alternative name for the degrees of perfection argument for the existence of God.

Henotheism. From the Greek henos ('one') and those ('god'). The view that one god is supreme, while not denying the existence of other gods. Often taken to be an intermediate stage between polytheism and monotheism.

Heraclitus of Ephesus (died after 480 BC). Greek philosopher known as 'the obscure', 'the riddler', and 'the weeping philosopher'. The most famous doctrine attributed to him had been that all things are in a state of flux; even the unchanging hills change, but more slowly than most other things.

Hereditary Property. A term used in formal logic. An R-hereditary property (where R is a relation) is any property P such that for any objects b and c, if c has the property p and b stands in the relation R to c, then b also has the property, p. For instance, if R is the relation 'is greater by three than' the property of being exactly divisible by three is R-hereditary among numbers, since, for any numbers b and c, if c is exactly divisible by three, and b is greater by three than c, then b is exactly divisible by three.

Heresy. From the Greek hairesis ('a taking for oneself,' 'choice,' 'sect'). In the religious tradition of the West the term has come to mean the denial of a revealed truth.

Hermeneutics. From the Greek hermeneutikos ('interpretation').

In its classical reference the term refers to the interpretation of texts, especially Biblical, but also philosophical.

In philosophy of the social sciences one view is that the social sciences are more akin in method to hermeneutics than to the laboratory sciences. Spranger, for example, viewed psychology as a 'hermeneutic of the spirit.'

In philosophy hermeneutics has joined Structuralism in creating a method of interpretation which centers philosophy once again in culture.

Hermeticism. The occult tradition based on the late antique treatises known by the collective title of the Corpus Hermeticum.

Herodotage. A colloquial name for anthropological literature in which human habits, customs, and beliefs are compared. The reference is to a confrontation, recorded by the Greek historian Herodotus, between rival commitments to burying, burning, or eating dead relations.

Heterological. Inapplicable to itself. For example, 'French' is heterological because it is not a French word (compare homological).

Heteronomy. From the Greek heteros and nomos meaning 'the rule of another.' Contrasted with autonomy the term is used by Kant to characterize ethical systems whose principles derive from a source outside the person. In the autonomous system of Kant the self determines itself by means of its own law. Tillich applied the term to a mode of specious reasoning which took its principles from outside itself.

Heuristic. Serving to indicate or stimulate investigation. In many cases it involves proceeding to a solution by trial and error in the absence of an algorithm. In modern logic, the word describes a process that may solve a particular kind of problem but offers no guarantee of success

Higher Order Logic. The study of validity in languages of second, or higher, order.

Hinduism 1500 B.C. to the Present. The native religious system of India. A religion without a founder, Hinduism reflects in itself the cultural history and social conditions of the Indian people from the time civilization flowered in the Indus Valley to our day. The various levels of religiou insight from magic to ethical idealism coexist in Hindu scriptures and practices.

Indeed, it is sometimes said that Hinduism is a Dharma (right action) instead of a religion. Conduct and belief here intermingle. Different modes of conduct and belief co-exist in Hinduism; the apparent inconsistencies which result may be moderated by the Hindu insight that the One expresses itself and is expressed in many ways. Accept the point and apparent polytheism of Hinduthought disappears for there are different ways of reaching the Supreme Being, and the gods are merely different names for the one God and different paths leading to the same goal. The Trimurti, or trinity, of later Hindu mythology, representing three aspects of the Supreme Being—Brahma, the creator; Vishnu the preserver; and Shiva the destroyer—is thus also consistent with a strict monotheism; as are the successions of divine incarnations which are said in the Bhagavad-Gita to occur wheneve 'the law fails and lawlessness uprises.' In any case, Hinduism is a natural growth characterized by richness but not a doctrine shaped into logical coherence.

(1) The scriptures of Hinduism, called Vedas, (meaning 'knowledge') consist of three parts : (a) the Samhitas (meaning 'collections') include the Rig-veda, a collection of hymns in praise of the gods; the Sama-veda, melodies relating to these hymns; the Yajur-veda sacrificial formulae; and the Atharva-veda, magical formulae; (b) the Brahamanas, texts dealing with ritual and sacrifice, their meaning and value; (c) the Upanishads, essentially philosophical discourses, and the primary source for insight into Hindu philosophy.

(2) Comparable to, although more vast in scope than, the position held in Greek culture by the Iliad and Odyssey are the Ramayana (q.v.) and the Mahabharata (q.v.). In process of formation throughout the 1st.

Hindu Philosophy. Just as it is impossible satisfactory to define Hinduism as a religion, no definition of what is typically Hindu philosophy is possible. It can only be described as those forms of philosophical thought that, regardless of their origins and original motivation, allied themselves with, and were accepred by, the very complex religious superstructure called 'Hinduism', which set itself in opposition to materialism, Jainism, and Buddhism. For most practical purposes, the Vedanta and Mimamsa alone are strictly 'Hindu', by virtue either of their adherence to the fundamental scriptures and rites of Hinduism, or simply because they were accepted as such by the Hindus (thus the advaita Vedanta of Sankara, strictly speaking. trons cends Hindu religion). The four other systems (Samkhya, Yoga, Nyaya, and Vaisesika), which Hinduism includes in its traditional list of six 'orthodox' systems (darsanas), are only nominally Hindu (or religious in the general sense of the word). In particular, the Vaisesika and the Nyaya differ far more from the Vedanta than do the Buddhist Madhyamaka or Vijnanavada.

Historical Explanation. A topic that has been the focus of considerable discussion and argument in the philosophy of history. Recent controversy, which echoes earlier disputes concerning the relations between the human studies and the natural sciences, has largely revolved round two opposed claims : the contention that such explanation conforms in its essential structure to explanations of the kind typified in scientific contexts, and the contrary contention that it is sui generis, being susceptible to a quite different pattern of analysis. Proponents of the first position, originally favoured by logical empiricists eager to uphold the unity of scientific method, have invoked the deductive-nomological (or covering law) model of explanation; an event is explained, in history as elsewhere, in so far as the assertion of its occurrence is derivable from premises comprising descriptions of initial conditions together with 'universal hypotheses' or laws. Proponents of the second, on the other hand, have stressed the crucial role played by notions like meaning and intention in the understanding of human behaviour: it is argued that these set historical accounts within a teleological or rational framework of interpretation that has no counterpart at the level of scientic thought and enquiry.

Historicism. From the German Historismus, a term signifying an emphasis (or overemphasis) on history. The term was introduced by Mannheim and Troeltsch and was from the start ambiguous. Applied usually to approaches such as that of Vico who asserted that "everything is history,' and Dilthey who argued that even historians are captive to the assumptions of the age in which they write, the net of its application is sometimes extended to Hegel, Marx, Croce, Collingwood, and Heidegger. When used pejoratively, the term is taken as an instance of the genetic fallacy, explaining a phenomenon away by reference to its origin.

History, Philosophy of. Two separate branches of enquiry, commonly distinguished as speculative and critical.

1. Speculative philosophy of history. Enquiry characteristically undertaken with the aim of providing an interpretation of the human past considered as a whole. Those who have embarked upon such an enterprise have regarded the course taken by history as conforming to some general order or design, the task of the philosopher (unlike that of the ordinary practising historian) being one of eliciting a comprehensive pattern in terms of which the historical process in its totality can be seen to have a 'meaning' or to exhibit an overall direction.

2. Critical philosophy of history. Enquiry primarily concerned, not with the human past itself, but with modes of thought and enquiry about that past. Thus it takes as its subject matter the categories in terms of which the historian seeks to comprehend and interpret his material and the presuppositions that underlie his procedures. As such, it is a second-order discipline, which in the first instance evolved in response to methodological issues arising from the proliferation of historical studies during the 19th century. The contention that history had finally taken shape as an autonomous form of thinking, distinguishable from other types of investigation but not for that reason inferior, was central to the work of continental philosophers such as Dilthey and Croce at the turn of the present century, and it was later to be given eloquent expression by the British writer, R.G. Collingwood.

Holism. 1. The contention that wholes, or some wholes, are more than the sum of their parts. One special version is organicism, urging that some systems that are not literally organisms are nevertheless crucially like organisms, whose parts can only be understood in relation to their functions in the complete and ongoing whole. 2. (in the social sciences and history). A theory that claims that society may, or should, be studied in terms of social wholes : that is, that the fundamental data of social analysis are not individuals or individual manifestations but rather societal laws, dispositions, and movements.

Homoiousian. From the Greek homoi ('like') and ousia ('substance'). The doctrine defeated in the Council of Nicaea and later that the Son is of similar, but not identical, essence or substance as the Father.

Homological Describing an association or similarity based on a correspondence in structure, origin, and development, though not necessarily in function. It is also used to express a particular relation that a word may have to itself, that is, when it applies to itself.

Homo Mensura. From Latin meaning 'man the measure.' The phrase applied to the doctrine of the Greek sophist, Protagoras that all standards and judgments are relative to man. The doctrine is sometimes interpreted as an individual and sometimes as a collective relativity.

Homonym. A word with the same form or sound as another but different in meaning, as pole (flag) and pole (magnetic) or bear (grizzly) and bear (children).

Humanism. A term employed in contrast to an opposing term, *e.g.*, 'absolutism,' 'theism,' in which human values and appreciations are presumably less central.

(1) The doctrine of Protagoras, taking men as the measure, stands in contrast to various types of absolutism, especially of an epistemological nature.

(2) In the Renaissance the term signified a return to the Greek sources and individual criticism and interpretation in contrast to the tradition of Scholasticism and religious authority.

(3) In more recent centuries the term has been often used in contrast to theism, locating in man the source of goodness and creativity. August Comte is an extreme example of this usage, having formalized an ecclesiastical framework for 'the worship of humanity'.

Humanity. From the Latin humanitas ('human nature, feeling, or kindness'). The term is less used in philosophy than is cognates although Stoicism in viewing man as a citizen of the cosmos had clearly arrived at the concept. One of the basic translations of jen in Confucianism is 'humanity.'

(1) In the final development of his point of view Comte called for a religion of humanity. Churches dedicated to this religion were established in a number of countries.

(2) Feuerbach (*q v.* 2) regarded humanity as unlimited and capable of achieving any quality, even though individual men are finite. Indeed, according to Feuerbach, men—beginning with this unlimited quality of humanity—have mistakenly projected the idea of God.

Hume's Fork. The increasingly popular nickname for an aggressive employment of Hume's fundamental distinction between propositions stating or purporting to state only 'the relations of ideas' and propositions stating or purporting to state 'matters of fact and real existence'. (Inquiry concerning Human Understanding (IV (i)). This distinction is substantially the same as that between truths of reason and truths of fact in Leibniz earlier.

Hume's Law. The increasingly popular label for Hume's insistence that the naturalistic fallacy is indeed a fallacy; and hence that conclusions about what ought to be cannot be deduced from premises stating only what was, what is, or what will be—and the other way about.

Hylomorphism. From the Greek hyle ('matter') and morphe ('form') The doctrine that all physical things have been composed of matter and form. Identified with Aristotle, the doctrine likewise characterizes Thomistic philosophy. Form is the principle of actuality and activity, while matter is the principle of potentiality and passivity.

Hylomorphism. The metaphysical doctrine that every natural object is somehow composed of matter and form. The character, relationship, and function of matter and form are central problems in the Physics and Metaphysics of Aristotle, and his solution, the doctrine of hylomorphism, was taken up by the scholastic philosophers, notably Aquinas. It was prominent in discussions of the relation of body and soul and of such theological enigmas as the nature of the Eucharist.

Hylozoism. From the Greek hyle ('matter') and zoe ('life'). A doctrine predicating life of all matter. Held by many early philosophers, among them Thales, suggestions of the view are to be found in most philosophies which find the world to be teleologically ordered. If all living forms are sentient to some degree, Hylozoism becomes a sub-class of Panpsychism.

Hypostasis. From the Greek term hypostasis, from hypo ('under') and hitasthai ('to stand').

(1) For Aristotle the individual substance in the perfection of its actuality.

(2) Aquinas applied the term to second substances which subsist in the species.

Hypothesis. From Newton onwards, a theory or suggestion that still has overtones of the arbitrary or the speculative. Sometimes, even after all reasonable doubt has been dispelled, a theory retains the title of a hypothesis (for example, Avogadro's hypothesis).

Hypothetical. Describing a valid syllogism consisting of two premises, both conditional in form, and a conditional conclusion. The three statements forming the argument contain between them just three distinct component propositions each of which appears twice, as for example in 'If the crops fail, the villagers will starve. If there is a drought, the crops will fail. Therefore, if there is a drought, the villagers will starve'.

Hypothetico-Deductive Method. The method of creating scientific theory by making an hypothesis (or set of hypotheses) from which results already obtained could have been deduced, and which also entails new experimental predictions that can be verified or refuted. There is controversy over the credit that accrues to such hypotheses when a prediction is verified. It is historically uncertain to what extent the method describes actual scientific procedure, where the fit between theory and observation often does not seem as tight as that of strict deducibility.

I

Icon. A sign that has some of the characteristics of that which it signifies, for example, a cloth sample or a portrait.

Idea. A Greek term, idea, originally meaning 'vision' or 'contemplation.' The Greek term eidos has the same root, and generally the same meaning.

The atomism of Leucippus and Democritus stressed the origin of ideation in sense-images (eidola), the usage continued by Epicurus The emphasis, if not the term, is continuous throughout the empirical tradition of Western philosophy.

For Plato (q.v. 1, 9) on the other hand, although he used both idea and eidos, ideas are not 'appearances' but the structural elements of things. Sensation may provide an initial clue to ideation, but ideas are thought, not sensed.

Idea-force Q.v. Fouillee.

Ideal. From the Greek idea ('vision' or 'contemplation'). Deriving from the term Plato used to designate the eternal ideas or forms, each of which was perfect of its kind, common usage has retained the valuational aspect of the word while discarding its epistemological or metaphysical aspect.

Ideal Evidence, Paradox of. A paradox which is affecting assignment of probability If a very small probability is assigned to an event, but on slender evidence, then ideal evidence could emerge that further justifies that low valuation. The paradox is that this evidence does not alter the probability assignment, yet it might make the observer more confident than before that the event will not happen.

Idealism. A name given to a group of philosophical theories, that have in common the view that what would normally be called 'the external world' is somehow created by the mind.

Ideatum. The object of, as well as that which is represented in the mind by, an idea.

Identity, Principle of. One of the three laws of thought, the principle—applied variously to statements and to things—holds that a proposition or a thing is identical with itself and implies itself. The principle is useful in logic and can in fact be demonstrated.

Identity Theory. The view that mental states and brain states are contingently identical. The claim is that this identity is not a matter of definition but scientific discovery.

Identity Theory of Mind. A materialist theory of consciousness which identifies being in such and such a state of consciousness with being in some corresponding neurophysiological state.

Identity Theory of Predication (or Truth). If predicates, like subjects, are ultimately noun phrases (the two-term theory) and name objects (the two-name theory), then sentences containing those predicates are true just if subject and predicate are names of the same thing. That is, whatever are named by subject and predicate are identical.

Ideology

1. Generally, any system of ideas and norms directing political and social action.
2. As used by Marx and Engels in The German Ideology, the word refers to such general systems only in so far as they

are recognized to contain falsehood and distortion generated by more or less unconscious motivations.

Idols of the Mind. The false assumptions and illusions, identified by Francis Bacon in Novum Organum Book I, 39–44, as the four main sources of error besetting the human mind in its pursuit of truth. These are :

(1) the idols of the tribe 'inherent in human nature and the very tribe or race of men, for man's sense is falsely asserted to be the standard of things';

(2) the idols of the den (or cave), which are peculiar to each individual;

(3) the idols of the market-place, 'formed by the reciprocal intercourse and society of man with man', particularly as a result of 'bad and unapt formation of words'; and

(4) the idols of the theatre, attributable to 'false philosophies.

Iff. An abbreviation for 'if and only if.' The abbreviation expresses material equivalence. 'P iff q' means 'if p then q, and if q then p ' It is thus a stronger form than material implication. 'Iff' performs the same function as the signs '≡' and '⇌' which are more usual in formal expressions.

Ignoratio Elenchi. A Latin phrase literally meaning 'reasoning from ignorance.' The ignoratio elenchi means 'irrelevant reasoning,' and applies to those cases where it is taken to establish some conclusion other than the one, if any, which can be deduced from its premises. It thus applies to the entire list of 'fallacies of relevance'.

Illation. The process of inferring a conclusion from a premise or premises, as well as the conclusion thus inferred.

Illicit Major. A fallacy associated with the categorical syllogism in traditional logic. It is committed when the major term is distributed in the conclusion but not in the premise.

Illicit Minor. A fallacy associated with the categorical syllogism in traditional logic. It is committed when the minor term is distributed in the conclusion but not in the premise.

Illocution. Refers to an utterance in which an illocutionary act (act done in speaking) is performed.

Illumination Divine. In the history of philosophy both truth and God have often been described in terms of light, and not seldom all three are merged in a single conception

Illusion. From the Latin illudere ('to illude,' *i.e.* 'to deceive, elude, delude'). In philosophy there are many doctrines holding that the world is not as it appears.

Illusion, Arguments From. The collective name given to all appeals, made for the purpose of casting doubt upon perceptual beliefs, to the possibility and actual occurrence of perceptual error. The term 'illusion' here covers much that would not in non-philosophical contexts be so called.

Imagination. Refers to a form of mental activity held to be distinct from cognitive or rational processes; a free, creative ordering of the contents of mind. Imagination in this sense is often confused with the production of mental imagery, which would be better called 'imaging'.

Imitation. A translation of the Greek term mimesis. The theory of imitation, treated under Mimesis, represents the application to aesthetics of the metaphysical theory of participation.

Immanence. From the Latin immanere ('to inhabit'). The term has been used of actions, principles, and in some doctrines of the relation between man and God.

Immanent. In-dwelling The word is often used by pantheists to describe the way in which God dwells in, or is in some sense identified with, the created world.

Immaterialism. A term created by Berkeley to characterize his position that there is no material substance.

Immortalist. Refers to a person who believes that somehow people, or some crucial elements in people, survive death and last for ever.

Immortality. The phrase 'of the soul' normally follows this term. By 'immortality of the soul' is meant the infinitely prolonged existence of that centre of awareness to which the term 'I' refers. The concept of immortality is usually viewed as Greek in origin an invention of Socrates or Plato, although it very quickly became an ,mportant part of much Christian faith. In Eastern thought the concept is also present, although it is subordinate to a conception of Nirvana in which self-identity is lost.

Imperative. The characteristic mood of the main verb in sentences (imperative sentences) with which conduct-guiding speech acts, such as requests and orders, are standardly performed. Imperatives, that is imperative sentences, are of interest to moral philosophers and logicians. One influential theory states that moral judgments imply imperatives, and hence that, for example, 'If you ought to do X, do it' is a valid inference when the 'ought' is a moral 'ought'.

Implication. A family of closely related notions, attempts to provide an adequate account of which have occupied many volumes. Problems arise when one seeks to determine relationships within the family, and, as a result, clear and agreed definitions are not available.

Implication is a notion that is left sitting between conditional statements on the one hand and entailment on the other, and as a rasult various 'kinds' or implication are distinguished in terms of their relation to these other notions. Material implication is the relation holding between A and B when the material conditional '$A \supset B$' is true.

Imposition' First and Second. In Scholastic logic, terms of first imposition consisted of terms of first and second intention. Terms of second imposition were grammatical terms, *e.g*, 'noun' 'pronoun,' 'verb,' etc.

Impossibility. In the everyday, colloquial sense, impossibility is always a matter of what—perhaps only in certain circumstances, or by certain people—simply cannot occur or simply cannot be done. In this sense what is naturally impossible, or impossible for men, or impossible for certain men in certain circumstances, would be for God at any time not merely possible but easy.

Impression Hume's term for the material of sensation. He divided impressions into simple and complex, leading to simple and complex ideas.

Imputation. In theology the attribution of guilt or merit to one person on the basis of the guilt or merit of another. The concept applies not only to the doctrine of original sin (q.v. 3) but also to that of justification by faith (q.v.).

Incarnation. From the Latin in and caro ('flesh'). The term usually refers to the doctrine that God has embodied, or will embody,

Himself in human from. The doctrine is held in numerous religions.

Incongruent (or incongruous) Counterparts. Another name for enantiomorphs.

Inconsistency. The negation of consistency :

1. In the traditional square of opposition a property of those propositions which cannot be affirmed together, *i.e.*, both contradictories and contraries.

2. In modern logic a set of propositions or propositional functions is said to be inconsistent if one can derive from the set anything whatever.

Inconsistent Triad. A set of three statements of which at least one must be false because from any two of them the negation of the third may be deduced. Where the deduction is syllogistic, this form of inconsistency is sometimes called an antilogism.

Incontinence. An alternative term for weakness of will or acrasia.

Incorrigible. Directly and conclusively verified, not subject to any further tests.

Index. For Peirce one of the three major classes or signs.

Indexical. An alternative name for token-reflexive.

Indian Materialism. A somewhat marginal but long-lived aspect of Indian philosophy, that appears under various labels, such as Carvaka, Lokayata, and Ajivika. None of the original writings of these schools, which flourished as early as c. 600 BC, are extant, and information about their teaching can be gained only from indirect accounts. In most materialist schools man is analysed purely in terms of material components and their inter-action. This analysis is usually connected with a pessimistic attitude; hedonism appears only quite rarely. The influence of this type of thinking was less philosophical (though the Vaisesika may exhibit it) than sociological, for the teaching was used in attacking ritul and mystical religion.

Indian Philosophy. Although Indian thought developed in an intellectual climate which in many ways was different from and almost certainly not influenced by, the ancient Greek world, abundant and often striking similarities with Western philosophical thought justify the application of the term 'philosophy' to it. The nature of the world-view taken for granted by the majority of schools and, in the course of time, an increasingly religious preoccupation nevertheless led Indian philosophy in a somewhat different direction from occidental.

Indicative. The characteristic moode of the main verb in ordinary statements and question.

Indicator Word (or term). An alternative name for a token-reflexive.

Indifference. From the Greek a ('not') and diaphoros ('different'). The term has been applied to a variety of philosophical problems.

Concerning value, for example, Stoics, Cynics, and Skeptics agreed in holding that one could not be indifferent to virtue and vice. Virtue was to be sought and vice avoided. But one should be indifferent with respect to all other attitudes and values.

Indifference, Principle of. The principle made prominent by Laplace, allowing us to regard events as equally probable if we can see no reason why one should occur rather than the other.

Indiscernibility of Identicals. The principle that if x and y are identical, then x has every property that y has, and y has every property that x has. The converse of the identity of indiscernibles, it is sometimes called Leibniz's law.

Individual. From the Latin individuals ('undivided or indivisible' translated from the Greek atomon ('indivisible').

In traditional logic the individual is the logical subject which admits of predicates, and cannot be predicated of anything else; *e.g.*, one says that man, is rational, not that rational is man. From Aristotle through Boethius (who intro duced into logic the Latin term individuum) into modern times this usage is current.

Individuality. A term which becomes prominent in 19th century Idealism, apparently as a corrective to emphases on absoluteness and the organic nature of society.

Individuation, Principle of. It signifies the principle by which a philosopher attempts to move in thought from the infima, or smallest, species to the individual member of that species.

Indra. The beneficient storm and fertility god of the Vedic religion. He wields the thunderbolt, brings rain, overcomes his enemies and shares the body with his friends.

Indubitable. An epistemological term which denotes the property of being certain, or beyond rational doubt. The indubitability of a proposition is not equivalent to its logical necessity, since some contingent propositions may also be said to be effectively beyond doubt.

Induction. From the Latin in and ducere ('to lead in'), first translated into the Latin probably by Cicero from Aristotle's term, epagoge. The widespread distinction between induction as an inference moving from specific facts to general conclusions, and deduction as moving from general premises to specific conclusions is no longer respectable philosophically. This distinction distinguishes one kind of induction from one kind of deduction. It is much more satisfactory to think of induction as probable inference and deduction as necessary inference.

Inevitability

1. Logical necessity; if *q* follows inevitably from p this simply means that it follows necessarily.

2. Contingent inescapability; if some occurrence is inevitable, this means that it will happen regardless of all attempts to prevent it.

Inference. From the Latin in and ferre ('to carry or bring'). In logic, the procedure of deriving conclusions from premises. If the conclusion follows from a single premise, the process is said to be one of immediate inference.

Inference, Immediate. The type of inference in which the conclusion follows from a single premise.

Inference, Rule of. A rule for the construction of arguments which says what may be inferred from one or more statements whose logical structure is specified.

Infinite. From the Latin in ('not') and finis ('boundary', 'limit', 'end'). Thus that without boundary, limit or end. Etymologically, the term is gained by negation of the term 'finite'. There are those, however, who would claim that the co ɩ ption of the infinite is prior to that of the finite. The conception of the infinite has been associated from the start with series of numbers, magnitudes, times. and spaces. The endlessness of such series provides one conception of infinity, and some hold this to be the basic meaning of the term.

Infinite Divisibility. A concept that many philosophers, from Zeno of Elea onwards, have considered to be impossible, since it supposedly leads to paradox. If, they have argued, a (finite-sized) existent is infinitely divisible, then it must consist of infinitely many parts. These must either have some size, or lack size and be nothing. If each part has some size or other, however minute, then the aggregate of an infinite number of these parts will be infinitely large. But if each part has no size, then the aggregate would have no size, that is the original existent would be made up of nothing.

Infinity. A notion used since the time of the ancient Greeks who applied it to substance. It also occurred in the paradoxes of Zeno of Elea. The concept of the infinite was vague, loosely being taken as 'that which has no beginning or end' or 'that which has no boundary, internal or external.

Innate Ideas. Ideas or knowledge in the mind prior to and independent of sense experience. For Plato, knowledge of the Forms derives from innate ideas which are accessible to memory (reminiscence, argument from). For Descartes, all principles of science and knowledge are founded on clear and distinct ideas, or incorrigible truths, which are innate in the mind and which may be captured by the method of reason.

Innateness. From the Latin in and natus ('born'). In philosophy the doctrine that ideas and principles are present in man from birth.

Inquiry. From the Latin in and quaero ('to seek').

Charles Peirce regarded inquiry as self-corrective, and more likely than any other method of having opinion lead to the truth.

For John Dewey inquiry is the heart of philosophic activity and the meaning of intelligence.

Inquisition. From the Latin inquirere ('to inquire'). An institution established within the Roman Catholic Church for the purpose of eliminating heresy, the Inquisition gained its distinctive form over a considerable period of time.

Inscription. A linguistic entity, like a sentence. The term figures in some analyses of propositional attitudes, for example, belief.

Instinct. In psychological theory, this term refers to an habitual pattern of behaviour that is innate or inherited rather than learned or acquired. The concept of instinct is particularly significant in Freud's psychological theory, where the libido is regarded as the reservoir of instinctual energy which issues in sexual or aggressive behaviour. In behaviourist theory, J.B. Watson distinguished instinctual patterns of responses from those that are conditioned or conditionable.

Instrumentalism. A theory of the nature of thought, logic, and acquisition of knowledge, advanced by Dewey, developing the pragmatism of William James. Ideas, concepts, and judgments are instruments functioning in experienced situations and determining future consequences. Propositions are to be regarded as means in the process of enquiry; as such, they cannot be true or false but are characterizable only as effective or ineffective. Judgments may have truth-values relative to whether or not their assertion is warranted. Ideas and practice work together as instruments : ideas relate experiences, making prediction possible, and are in turn tested by experience.

Insufficient Reason, Principle of. An alternative name for the principle of indifference.

Intellect. From the Latin intelligere ('to understand'). The power or faculty of knowing as compared to will or feeling.

Intentionality. From the same root as the term, intension.

Interactionism. Refers to a dualistic theory of the relation between mind and body, according to which physical events can cause mental events, and *vice versa.* Examples have been feeling an emotion making the heart beat faster, or a piece of music causing a poignant memory. Mind-body problem.

Intrinsic Value. Correlate of extrinsic value. The phrase applies to states of being or experience valuable in themselves without regard to their consequences. 'Final value' is a synonymous expression.

Inter Finitum Et Infinitum Non Est Proportio. (Latin for : there is no proportion between infinity and finitude.) A maxim with an important bearing on Pascal's wager.

Interpretation. The assigning of meanings to the expressions of a formal language. Any language can be treated as a system of symbols in which sentences, and other kinds of expression, are constructed according to syntactical rules (rules of grammar). To do this is to ignore any meaning that the expressions of the language might have; it is to treat the symbols as constituting an uninterpreted structure or formal language.

Intersubjectivity. Refers to the property of holding in reference to more than one subject, rather than purely subjectively.

Introspection. Awareness by an individual of his own states and condition, with particular reference to his mental and emotional activity.

Intuition. A form of uninferred or immediate knowledge.

Intuitionism

1. (in ethics) The view that (at least some) moral judgments are known to be true by intuition.
2. The view that there are several distinct moral duties, that cannot be reduced to one basic duty, in contrast, for example, to utilitarianism. While both views can be, and are, held separately, they often go together.

Intuitionistic Logic. The logic employed and developed by intuitionistic mathematicians. It arises out of a view concerning the way in which meaning can be conferred on mathematical statements.

Inventio Medii. (Latin for : discovery of the middle.) The formal name for the logical pons asinorum.

Ionic Philosophy. The school of philosophy arising in Ionia during the 6th century B.C., originating the development of Greek philosophy.

Ishtar. Babylonian and Assyrian goddess. Also known as Astarte and Ashtoreth. Goddess of springs, vegetation, the universe of flocks and herds, sexual love, wedlock and maternity, she also bore a negative aspect as the destroyer of life, goddess of storm and war.

Islam. Name of the religion founded by Mohammed. 'Messenger of God, what is Islam ?' The prophet replied, 'Islam is to believe in God and His Prophet, to say the prescribed prayers, to give alms, to observe the feast of Ramadan, and to make the pilgrimage to Mecca.'

Islamic Philosophy. Early Islamic philosophy is characterized by a profound tendency towards syncretism. The theological simplicity of the nascent Islamic religion, which prevailed during the lifetime of its founder, the prophet Muhammad (570–632), later suffered an assault from such diverse elements as Iraqi gnosticism, Christian Hellenism, Persian dualism, and Greek thought. The easily understood profession of the Islamic faith, 'There is no god but God and Muhammad is His prophet", was confronted with the concepts and dialetic of Greek philosophy. These last manifested themselves as possible means to the solution of problems that swiftly arose in early Islamic thought. So the study of Islamic philosophy in its early stages is inevitably the study of the influence of Greek philosophy on Islam. Furthermore, philosophy and theology are inextricably mingled.

Isolationism Refers to a theory of aesthetic interpretation that holds a work of art may, or should, be understood without reference to its cultural and historical context.

Isomorphic. Having the same structure, due to resemblance between corresponding parts. The term is applicable in relating material objects, social organizations, works of art, and abstract concepts.

Isomorphism. From the Greek iso ('equal') and morphe ('form'). Although the conception of isomorphism has applicability to many areas of science, its relevance to philosophy derives from the discipline of mathematics, and relates to the close association between mathematics and logic. Any two groups of entities may be said to be isomorphic when they have the same structure, that is, when by a one-to-one correspondence the elements of one group can be correlated with the elements of the other. The concept has important applications throughout modern mathematics

J

Jacobites. Name by which the members of the Syrian National Church are known.

Jain Philosophy. Jainism is an Indian religion founded in the 5th century BC by the 'Jina' (conqueror) Mahavira. Its philosophy combines archaic Indian nature-philosophical speculations (compare Vaisesika) with the quest for liberation from the cycle of rebirth. It soon became ossified but it is possible to point to some creative thinkers, like Kundakunda (4th century AD).

The Jain system is presented under seven headings :

(1) Lifeless substances (ajiva), comprising space, the media of movement (dharma) and rest, time, and matter (pudgala), which consists of homogeneous atoms.

(2) An infinite number of souls (jiva). Essentially possessed of unlimited knowledge, power, and bliss, the souls become deprived of these qualities through.

(3) the influx (asrava) of subtle matter on accounts of words, thoughts, and deeds. Weighed down by it, the souls suffer

(4) bondage (bandha) in the world of phenomena, in the form of transmigration.

(5) refusing to allow further matter to enter (samvara), and

(6) exterminating (nirjara) the already present matter by means of a strict ethical discipline and severe penance, the soul obtains

(7) liberation (moksa), and moves upwards to the top of the universe.

Japanese Rligion and Philosophy. As in India and China, religion and philosophy in Japan have not been sharply differentiated until recent years. The native religion of Japan, Shinto goes back at least 2000 years although it was not named until Buddhism was introduced from China in the 6th century A.D. Confucianism had been introduced in the 5th century A.D. along with Chinese script.

(1) Confucian influence reached its height in the Tokugawa era (1603-1867). The neo-Confucian philosophers Chu Hsi and Wang Yang-Ming have received special attention and esteem.

(2) All the schools of Buddhism, developed in China, have been imported into Japan. The T'ien-T'ai School gave rise to the most powerful Japanese sect, the Nichiren; and the meditation school of Ch'an or Zen Buddhism has achieved a development in Japan far beyond anything it had achieved in China.

(3) Following the Meiji restoration of 1868, Japan was opened to Western philosophy with the result that Hegel, Eduard Von Hartmann, Windelband, Rickert, T.H. Green, William James, and John Dewey, exercised influence. From the mid-twenties the power of Marxism has steadily grown; and from the mid-forties the influence of existentialism has been increasing.

Jen. (Chinese for : humanity and benevolence) The basic principle of Confucius' moral and social philosophy.

Jewish Philosophy. A concern with the ultimate questions of the nature of the Universe and the human condition has been characteristic of Judaism from its beginnings. There has, however, always been a plurality of approaches determined to a large extent by the historical conditions governing Jewish life and the external influences that have operated on Jewish thought. Like Chrisitanity and Islam, Judaism represents a constructive synthesis of biblical monotheism and Greek philosophy. There has been considerable reciprocal influence between thinkers of the three Mosaic religious traditions.

Jnana. In Hinduism the way of knowledge. Correspondingly, Jnana Yoga is that one of the four types of yoga stressing knowledge as the path to liberation.

Judaism The religion of the Jewish people, parent religion of both Christianity and Mohammedanism. We shall consider Judaism in itself, and in terms of the philosophies developed within its framework.

Religiously, the origin of Judaism is usually traced to a compact between God and Abraham to foster the development of a special people in exchange for their devotion. In fact, this perspective must be associated with the time of the Babylonian exile; at least it was during that period that it was possible to conceive the history of this people as a series of triumphs and defeats, related to their faith and faithlessness in God. And since this view of history is present in the Bible, these are the people of the Book in an unique sense. Be this as it may, the intimate relation of God to the community accounts for the early history of Judaism as presenting an example of theocracy.

Judgment. From the Latin jus (right') and dicere ('to determine or say'). The current usage of the term is roughly synonymous to 'proposition'.

But as Aristotle used his terms in De Interpretatione, a proposition is a significant assertion, either true or false, resulting from a judgment. And when the spoke of the relations of opposition among significant assertions it was of contradiction and contrariety among 'propositions,' for example.

Justice. From the Latin jus ('right' or 'law'). In philosophy, the most influential analyses of the term were given by Plato and Aristotle

(1) The context for Plato's analysis was set by the Sophists who contrasted natural and conventional justice, usually preferring the former. Thrasymachus defined justice as the 'interest of the stronger.'

(2) Plato moved beyond the natural-conventional dichotomy, viewing justice in functional terms as the supreme virtue of the state, referring to the condition in which everyone is having and doing what in his own, andnot interfering in that which is another's.

(3) Aristotle held justice to be a mean between the injustice of interfering with what belongs to another, and suffering interference one's self. He distinguished between two forms of justice : distributive—one's just share of the resources of the state; and retributive—the redress of injury.

(4) Aquinas and Locke agree that there is a natural and rational order, identifiable with equity or justice, discernible through the exercise of reason.

Justification by Faith. In Christianity, the problem of how one is absolved, or acquitted, of his past actions, or how he acquires his new belong as a Christian.

K

Kaddish. An Aramaic term meaning "holy." A Jewish prayer with the same opening phrases as the Lord's Prayer. Since the Middle Ages the mourner's declararation of faith.

Kabbalah. (Hebrew for: tradition.) The mystical Jewish tradition in general, and in particular the theosophical system whose classical text is the Zohar. Jewish mysticism has its roots in antiquity, and shows strong signs of gnostic influence. Its two main preoccupations were cosmogony (Ma'aseh Bereshith) and the nature of God (Ma'aseh Merkabah); it also had a practical side, aiming at wonder-working and especially the artificial creation of a man.

Kafir. An Arabic term meaning "infidel." A term applied by Moslems to all unbelievers.

Kalam. (Arabic for : speech.) In Islamic philosophy the adducing of philosophical proofs to justify religious doctrine. The word is often translated as 'Muslim scholastic theology'; those who practised it were called 'mutakallimun'.

Kali. Hindu goddess. Wife of Shiva. Worshipped as the great and terrible mother, her cult has in the past led at times to human sacrifice. Wearing a necklace of skulls, dead bodies for earrings and a girdle of snakes, she greets her devotees with open mouth and protruding fang-like teeth.

Karaites. Hebrew term meaning "Reader of Scriptures." The term applies to a Jewish sect, centering in Babylon, rising in the 8th century A.D. The group repudiated the Talmud and accepted the Old Testament as sole authority. The movement, flourishing between the 9th and 12th centuries, stimulated defenses of the Talmudic tradition by the Rabbinic group. The sect still continues but with little influence.

Karma. From the Sanskrit kri which means "deed" or "action." The structure of one's life as resulting from one's prior actions in earlier existences. The view, then, requires reincarnation or metempsychosis as its complement.

In Hinduism karma (karma vidhi) is "the way of works." The object of works is to deal with the fact that the soul or self transmigrates, carrying its burden of karma, or effects.

In Jainism karma characterizes reality even down to the atomic level and the concept of "karmic matter" is central.

Kenosis. From the Greek kenoss which means "empty" The term begins in a Christological dispute centering around Philippians 2.7 where Christ is said to have "emptied himself, taking the from of a servant." According to some this means that Christ divested himself of his divine attributes during his earthly career. According to others the attributes were retained, although hidden from view.

Kepler (or Keppler). Johannes (1571—1630). German astronomer, who studied at Tubingen, taught mathematics at Graz and Linz, and worked under Tycho Brahe.

Kerygma. A Greek term which means the "good news," or "gospel." The New Testament message of salvation.

Keynes. John Maynard, 1st Baron Keynes (1883—1946). British economist, son of J.N. Keynes. His General Theory of Employment, Interest and Money (1936) was revolutionary, and policies supposedly derived from it guided or misguided many countries until a counte-revolution got under way in the 1970s.

Keynes wrote an important philosophical work A Treatise on Probability (1921) on probality and induction, in which he argued that probability attaches only to propositions (rather than events), and is objective in that a proposition always has a certain probality, independently of our recognition of it.

Khorda Avesta. One of the five parts of the Avesta, sacred scriptures of Zoroastrianism.

King. In the medieval doctrine of the two swords the temporal, in contrast to the spiritual, power. For John Wycliffe the king was God's vicar on earth. The doctrine of the Divine Right of Kings in the 17th century regarded the monarch as possessing spiritual, as well as temporal, authority.

Kingdom of God. A Hebrew concept which looked to the future for the fulfillment of God's rule over mankind. Jesus began his ministry with the announcement that the kingdom was at hand, picturing it both as already present and as imminent.

Kismet. An Arabic term which means 'fate'.

Knowledge. Philosophical questions about the nature of knowledge belong either to epistemology or to the philosophy of mind (mind, philosophy of). The two groups of questions may be roughly separated by saying that the first group concentrates on the nature of knowledge, whereas the second concentrates on the nature of the knower.

Karon. From the Arabic Qur'an, from qara'a meaning 'to read.' Hence, the meaning is 'the reading' or 'the lesson'. The sacred book of Islam had its origin in 622 A D. when, after the migration to Medina. Mohammed bagan to dictate his oracles to a disciple as they were revealed Part of the contents of the Koran derive from the Mecca period (prior to 622); the rest belong to the period from 622 to 632. On Mohammed's death the Karon existed in scattered fragments, even though many Moslems knew large sections by heart. The caliph Abu Bekr assigned to Zaid ibu Thabit the task of collecting all of the parts. The copy made by Zaid had no canonicity and other copies had been made. Othman, a later caliph, appointed Zaid and three others to collect all the copies and prepare a text which would be made universally binding. Having done this, all other available codices were destroyed. The result was the Koran. The redactors arranged the chapters, or suras, in an order discriminated only by length. The lonser suras were at the beginning, and the shorter toward the end.

Krishna. Along with Rama one of the last two incarnations of Vishnu. Their followers constitude a considerable portion of the Hindu people and a majority of the Vishnuites. Krishna is acknowledged as the supreme God in the Mahabharata, the Harivamsa and the Puranas, yet his actions reveal a Rajput Chieftain willing to employ questionable means for the sake of personal ends. Supposing that Krishna, the incarnate God, grew from the figure of the chieftain, how did this happen ? The path is somewhat complex. In the Vedic period, Krishna, having begum as a tribal head, is regarded as a wise man seeking religious truth. Vasudeva is mentioned quite early as a God mystically identical with Vishnu. It hapened that Krishna become identified with Vasudeva, thus taking over his identification with Vishnu, and thus did a Rajput chieftain become an incarnate God.

Kshatriyas. The warrior class in Indian tradition.

Kumarjiva. 344-413. Chinese Buddhist philosopher. Half-Indian and half-Chinese, Kumarajiva became a monk at the age of seven. He became so influential that kings sent armies to bring him to their courts. The title of 'National Teacher' was conferred on him. More than 1000 monks attended his daily lectures. In ten years he translated 72 Buddhist books into Chinese. He introduced the Middle Doctrine of Nagarjuna (*q v.*) into China. Among these were the really philosophical Buddhist texts. Hence, he made systematic philosophizing about Buddhism possible.

Kyrie Eleison. A Greek phrase which means 'Lord have mercy.' One of the few Greek phrases used in the Roman Mass and the Anglican Communion service, it is of course used in the litanies of the Eastern Church. Its presence in the Western rites may point to a common, vanished litany.

L

Lamaism. The system of religious and political doctrine which from the 15th to the 20th centuries ruled Tibet with spiritual influence; also in Mongolia, China, and Siberia. In the middle of the 15th century, to begin the story halfway through, the emperor of China (who also controlled Tibet) named two Buddhist monks to be, one the spiritual ruler and the other the temporal ruler of Tibet. The spiritual ruler was called the Dalai Lama; the temporal ruler the Pantshen Lama. The reason for the move was that this particular sect of Buddhism, a reform movement, had become astonishingly powerful in numbers and influence The two Grand Lamas are regarded as incarnations of celestial beings; the Dalai Lama of Avaiokitesvara, the Pantshen Lama of Amitabha. When either Lama died it was the duty of the other to discover the child in whom the bothisattva had become reincarnate. The names of all male children born shortly after the death of his counterpart would be laid before him. He would choose three names; a council of holy men after a week of prayer would select by lot one of the three to be the future Grand Lama.

Language Game. A key concept in the later work of Wittgenstein. According to his famous analogy between using language and playing games, we have in both various sets of rules or conventions, and these determine what moves are permissible or impermissible, successe or failuress, each set of rules indentifying a distinct game. A given move can be judged only according to the rules of the game to which it belongs. Many time-honoured philosophical problems result from judging moves in one game by the rules of another, and can be dissolved only by systematic clarification of the relevant differences; hence such clarification should be philosophy's main concern.

Lapouage Philonophy of. The phrase covers a variety of activities.

1. Philosophers interested in problems, for example, about mind and knowledge, may frame their questions in various ways. They may ask directly about mind or knowledge; they may talk about the concept of mind or knowledge; or they may begin by asking how the words 'mind' and 'knowledge' are used.

2. The procedure of investigating philosophical questions by reflecting on the uses of words generates another meaning of 'philosophy of language'. Here there are two questions. First there is a general question about the justifiability of approaching philosophical questions via a study of how word are used. Second, philosophers who study the use of words use such key terms as 'meaning', 'reference', 'truth', and use.

Law Philosophy of.

1. The analysis of the nature of law and legal systems; analytic jurisprudence.
2. The critical evaluation of the basis of legal authority and of the moral rationale behind legal decision making; ethical jurisprudence.

Law. In a descriptive sense "law" means "law of nature." an invariant relationshly found in phenomena by scientific investigation, and thus presumed to hold in the natural world.

Laws of Nature. Principles that may be either prescriptive or descriptive, but must always be in some sense necessary.

1. The prescriptive law of nature is conceived as a basic system of moral norms, the necessity of obedience being moral.

2. Descriptive laws of nature are supposed to hold with a (non-logical) necessity, and cannot be broken : a genuine exception would show only that what had been thought to hold as such a law does not.

Laws of Thought. In traditional logic one finds stated three principles upon which all logical thinking is held to depend. These are the laws or principles of identity, excluded middle, and contradiction. In modern logic the principles turn out to be tautologies.

Lazy Sophism. The nickname used by Leibnix and others for the argument that, since from 'X will be' it follows necessarily that 'X will be', therefore it must also follow that 'X' necessarily and inevitably will be'.

Learning Paradox. Refers to an old problem which was raised in Plato's Socratic dialogues and later found in some writings on education and certain medieval approaches to the knowledge of the nature of God. A person can learn only that which he doesn't know, but if he doesn't know it, how does he know what he is seeking to learn?

Least Number Principle. The principle that if a property or condition holds for some number then there is a least number that satisfies the condition. This principle is equivalent to the principle of complete induction.

Legalism. (Chinese fa chia : the school of law.) A school of thought that flourished in the state of Ch'in The policies of this school were instrumental in the unification by that state of the central Chinese kingdoms in 221 BC. The leading theorists, Shang Yang (d. 330 BC) and Han Fei (d. 233 BC) rejected all traditional moral values, making utility to the state the supreme criterion. Through a system of rewards and punishments, set out in a rigid code of law, all human activity was directed towards increasing the power of the state and its ruler, both internally and externally. To this end, the people were set to pursuing only agriculture and warfare, and all alternative forms of social activity were prohibited

Leibniz's Law. The principle that if one thing is identical with another then anything that is true of the one must also be true of the other. This sounds obviously true.

Lenin, Vladimir Ilyich. 1870-1924. Russian Marxist. Born in Simbirsk (now Ulianov). Studied at Kazan and St. Petersburg.

Imprisoned for revolutionary activity in 1895. Exiled to Siberia in 1897. It exile most of the time between 1900 and 1917. Headed the Soviet Union from 1917-24.

Principal writings : Materialism and Empirio-criticism (T), 1909; Imperialism (T), 1916; State and Revolution (T), 1917.

Lenin dedicated himself to the Marxist philosophy. In this regard his quest was to discover the strongest version of that philosophy He began with a Marxism closely oriented to that of Marx himself, abjuring the dialectic, while adhering to materialism. He ended, however, in agreeing with all of the propositions of Engels, while contributing a proposition, or at least a clarification, of his own 4.

LI. Chinese term meaning "propriety, "good manners." One of the cardinal virtues in Confucianism Li is the outward expiession of an inner harmony.

Liar Paradox. A paradox traditionally attributed to Empimenides the Cretan and supposedly strengthened by Eubulides. The statement, 'I am lying', is true only if it is false, and false if it is true.

Libertarianism

1. The view, opposed to determinism, that certain human actions'are not (or not entirely) governed by necessitating causal laws.

2. Whole-hearted political and economic liberalism, opposed to any social and legal constraints on individual freedom.

Liberty. From the Latin libertas, from libero ("to set free, liberate"). The term, like freedom has two senses : one is the metaphysical capacity to make decisions freely; the other is the social fact of having a certain amount of elbow-room within society.

Life, Human. The concept of human life is implicit in all philoso phical and religious discussion.

In Hinduism life is divided into a succession of four stages (ashramas), each with its duties and expectations.

Light. The analysis of light through much of the history of philosophy has been at the same time physical and divine illumination. The Neoplatonic doctrine treated light in dual terms.

Likelihood. In connection with a statistical hypothesis on a body of data, the chance of those data occurring if the hypothesis is true.

Limited Independent Variety, Principle of. The name given by J.M. Keynes to the contention that to justify inductive generalizations it has to be assumed "that the objects in the field, over which our generalizations extend, do not have an infinite number or independent qualities".

Linguistic Philosophy. An approach to philosophy that holds that a careful study of how language is actually used, taught, and developed in everyday discourse can illuminate, and even transform or dissolve, time-honoured philosophical problems.

Locution. A grammatically well formed and meaningful utterance. A locutionary act is the use of a locution to say something.

Logic. In its broadest sense logic is the study of the structure and principles of reasoning or of sound argument. Hence it is also a study of those relations in virtue of which one thing may be said to follow from or be a consequence of another.

Logical Atomism. The philosophy expressed in Wittgenstein's Tractatus Logico-philosophicus, written during World War I, and in a number of comtemporary papers by Russell. The belief was that analysis of the conditions necessary to give a sentence a definite meaning reveals that oridinary (molecular) sentences (or propositions) must be compounded from fundamental (atomic) units of meaning.

Logical Constants. Symbols that represent certain of the devices, independent words, prefixes, suffixes, and inflections in any language that enable one to discern the grammatical structure of a sentence

Logical Construction. A term used by philosophers, such as Russell and Wisdom, to characterize those things whose status and/or existence we are in doubt about or find problematic.

Logical Fiction. An object that is only apparently invoked by a sentence.

Logical Form. The form of an argument which is expressed in a symbolic representation from the structure of which the reasoning procedure adopted is apparent.

Logically-black-is-white Slide. The abusive nickname for the fallacy of arguing that, because the difference between two extremes is a difference of degree, therefore those extremes are really the same.

Logically Perfect Language. Refers to a language in which logical and grammatical structure entirely coincide.

Logically Private Language. Refers to a language in which all words must be defined in terms of the logically private experience of the individual language user.

Logically Proper Name. A proper name of the kind required by Russell's logical atomism.

Logical Paradoxes. Usually distinguished from the semantic paradoxes in that they can be expressed using only logical or set-theoretic terms.

Logical Positivism. The point of view of the Vienna Circle of Logical Positivists. The goal of the school, also known as "logical empiricism," was to purify philosophy—sifting out its metaphysical elements, and reconstituting the discipline with logic as its organon. The goal of philosophy in this sense is working out the implications of the logic of science.

Logical Subject. The subject of a sentence expressed in a logically perfect language, or the object that subject denotes.

Logistic Method. The method of studying a subject by formalizing it.

Logos. A Greek term meaning "reason, word, speech, discourse, definition, principle, or ratio." The function of the term in philosophy has turned largely on the logos as "reason."

Lokayata. The Indian philosophical doctrine that holds that this world is the only one that exists and that there is no after-life.

Lottery Paradox. Refers to a paradox which is arising from the principle that a rational man who believes each of two propositions ought to believe their conjunction But suppose there is a lottery with one hundred tickets 1,2,3,...100 A rational man may, it is said, believe that 1 will not win, 2 will not win, and so on for each ticket. So he ought, by the principle, to believe the conjunction of all these, which is equivalent to believing that no ticket will win. But one will ! So the natural principle of combining rational beliefs has a false consequence.

Love. The Latin terms are amnr and caritas, and the principal Greek terms are philia, eros, and agape. Philia developed the connotation of the kind of love involved in friendship (jen standing as the Chinese synonym), amor and eros the type of love based on desire, and caritas and agape the sense of a higher or selfless type of love.

Lowenheim-skolem Proofs. Leopold Lowenheim proved in 1915 that if 'E' is a well-formed formula of the first-order predicate calculus with certain predicate variables, then either not-F is provable or F can be satisfied in the natural number series by suitable determinations of the predicate variables.

Lowenheim-skolem Theorem. The proof, provided by Lowenheim in 1915, that any finite set T of sentences which has a model, has a denumerable model, which result Skolem generalized in 1920 to the case where T is a denumerably infinite set of sentences.

Loyalty. For Royce the ideal of loyalty is a universal, capable of bringing harmony among competing loyalties. The principle of ethics is, from this perspective. "Be loyal to loyalty".

L-truth. For a discussion of L-true and L-false sentences where 'L' stands for "logically," and discussion of L-determinate and L-indeterminate concepts.

Lyceum. The public garden in Athens that gave its name to the school of philosophy founded by Aristotle in 335 BC.

M

Macrocosm. From the Greek makros ('great') and kosmos ('universe'). The term is contrasted with microcosm, from mikros ('small') and kosmos ('universe'). Macrocosm, taken to refer to the universe, is set in contrast to man, the microcosm, a little universe.

Madhva 1197-1276. India Vedantan philosopher. Along with Shankara and Ramanuja, one of the chief commentators on Vedanta philosophy. A dualist (or pluralist), he opposed Shankara's non-dualism. His radical pluralism separated him from Ramanuja. His position is much indebted to the Sankhya school of Indian philosophy.

Principal writings : Commentary on the Vedanta Sutras (T).

Madhyamika. One of the four chief philosophical schools of Buddhism, the system of the Mean or 'middle way.' Members of the school are called Madhyamikas. Negarjuna is regarded as its founder. The school of Shunyavada was highly influential in shaping Mahayana Buddhism. Chi-Tsang continued the development of the school in China.

Magnitudes. A magnitude is intensive if it is possible to order things of a certain type according to it; it is extensive if it is both intensive and different numerical values can be assigned to differing positions in the ordering, such that the ordering by magnitude is preserved when ordered by the relation 'less than'.

Mahabharata, the. The great Brahman epic poem of the 6th century B.C., which contains the Bhagavad-Gita as one of its parts, the Mahabharata tells the story of/two families, both having claims upon the throne, involved in struggle. In addition to the themes of the Bhagavad-Gita, the poem contains an elaboration of :

1. The four aims of life : righteousness, wealth, worldly enjoyment and spiritual freedom.

2. The four Ashramas, or the four stations of life and their duties : the student, householder, forest-dweller, and ascetic.

3. The four castes : Brahmin (priest and teacher), Kshatriya (warrior), Vaisya (merchant), Sudra (laborer).

Mahat. Sankhya (5a).

Mahavira. Vardhamana.

Mahayana Buddhism. Buddhism, Mahayana.

Mahdi. From the Arabic meaning 'the guided, or well-directed, one.' The one who will appear on earth as Allah's representative to lead the hosts of Islan to world-wide victory. He will be the finall Imam.

Maieutic. From the Greck maia ('midwife'). Normally used as an adjective, describing Socrates method of delivering an individual of his ideas.

Maitreya. The expected or future Buddha, prophesied by Gautama Buddha whose incarnation will spread the doctrine, restore the good society, and save all beings. According to the prophecy Maitreya is to come in 5,670,000,000 years.

Major Premise. In a categorical syllogism, the premise containing the major term.

Major Term. The predicate term of the conclusion of a categorical syllogism.

Man. Since philosophy is the work of man, all of its basic divisions, Epistemology, Ethics, Aesthetics, etc., comment upon his nature.

Plato regarded man as essentially a tripartite unity of mind, will, and passions.

Hsun Tzu regarded man as naturally evil, and thus requiring the pressures of outward discipline.

Manichaelsm. A religious movement named after its Persian founder Mani, 'the apostle of God' (c. 216-76 AD).

Manifold. (German : manningfaltigkeit) A term usen by Kant, in the first Critique, to mean the various and discrete elements of sensory experience—that which is presented to the senses and which the mind then organizes through concepts, in order to perceive the world (as made up of material objects and so on).

Mantra. A Sanskrit term meaning 'counsel' or 'instrument of though.' In the Vedas the term refers to hymns and prayers to the gods, as well as to ritualistic or devotional formulae.

Many Questions, Fallacy of. A mistake which consists of putting or accepting a question that tacitly takes for granted a false or at least disputations answer to some prior question or questions. It is a common form of intellectual error, though not perhaps in the strictest sense a fallacy.

Many-sorted Logic. Refers to the study of validity in many-sorted languages. A formal language with predicate structure is many-sorted if typographically distinct kinds of names and variables are used with the intention that interpretation of the language will involve assigning, to each kind, different categories of objects for their universes of discourse.

Many-valued Logic. Refers to the study of validity and consequence under an interpretation that assigns three or more possible values to the sentences of a formal language.

Marburg School. One of the most important divisions of Neo-Kantianism. Founded by Hermann Cohen (1842-1918) and Paul Natorp (1854-1924), the Marburg school was mainly concerned with philosophy of science.

Marx, Karl (1818-83). German social theorist, interested mainly in economics and history. He had little to do with the philosophical doctrines that now form part of Marxism. In the first volume of Das Kapital (1867) Marx made use of, and to some extent discussed, a theory of method that owed something to Hegel. Marx called this a dialectical method, but said that it turned Hegel's dialectic the right way up, in that it was materialistic and not idealistic. But though Marx's dialectic may in a broad sense be called a philosophy of history, it is really an account of socio-historical development rather than a philosophical theory, and so is the concern of the historian rather than of the philosopher.

Marxism (or Classical Marxism). The body of doctrines originally propounded by Marx and Engels, which involves certain philosophical views. These views (propounded mainly by Engels) rely heavily on the philosophy of Hegels, and in particular on his thesis that change has to be explained in terms of contradiction. But whereas Hegel's philosophy is a form of idealism, Marxism declares itself to be a form of materialism. Not, however, 'mechanistic' materialism, but dialectical' materialism, where due weight is given to 'the transformation of quantity into quality'. This means that mind is not reduced to matter but is seen as coming from matter, though qualitatively different from it.

Masked Man Fallacy. Refers to the mistake of arguing that because someone knows (or does not know) something under one description, they must therefore know it (or they therefore cannot know it) as the same thing when it appears under another description.

Mass Noun. A term which refers to an uncountable thing. Glasses of water can be counted, water cannot. Hence water is a mass noun.

Materialism. Any set of doctrines stressing the primacy of material over spiritual factors in metaphysics, value theory, physiology, epistemology or historical explanation.

Mathematics, Philosophy of. The study of the concepts of and justification for the principles used in mathematics.

Although mathematics is a useful tool in science, few believe that the subject matter of mathematics is physical objects or that empirical observation is the ultimate ground for deciding the truth or falsity of mathematical statements.

Matter. Refers to that which has traditionally been contrasted either with form or with mind.

Maxim. In ordinary language a rule of action, summing up wisdom in an established context. In Kant, a rule providing ethical guidance.

Maya. From the Sanskrit maya ('magic') The term is used in Indian philosophy to refer to the world as an appearance, somehow different from the reality. Indian philosophy contains a range of possible interpretations of the status of the world. On the one extreme of this range, Ramanuja, holds the world to be perfectly real, although finite; at the other extreme

Shankara as a representative of the Advaita Vedanta holds the world to be an outright illusion.

Mean, Doctrine of the. In the ethics of Aristotle the doctrine that virtue lies between extremes (although closer to excess than to deficiency).

In Chinese philosophy the Middle Way or Chung Yung in which every feeling is exercised in its proper degree and in harmony with every other.

In Buddhist philosophy the strategy whereby desire is eliminated and Nirvana gained.

Meaning. Theories of meaning are formulated through determining a position on the significance and interrelations of sense-data, words and sentences, the use of words and sentences in ordinary language, ideas, and the problem of reference in regard to words, sentences, and ideas.

Meaning Postulates. Devices used by Rudolf Carnap to introduce analytic sentences into a formal language. Under all interpretations for a formal language L, only logical truths (such as 'No married woman is not married') will remain true invariantly. Analytically true sentences (such as 'All spinsters are not married') will not, however, remain true under all interpretations, since their truth depends on the particular meanings of their non-logical words (such as 'married' and 'spinster').

Mechanical Explanation. An expression employed with different and often rather vague connotations, to cover various substantially different areas of denotation.

Mechanism

1. A scientific philosophy developed principally by Descartes. In place of the traditional scholastic kind of scientific explanation which invoked 'real qualities', Descartes claimed that his science was 'like mechanics in that it considers merely shapes, sizes, and motions.'

2. The thesis that genuine scientific explanation involves a search for mechanical models. Such models, based on known processes, describe the true mechanisms underlying the phenomenon to be explained.

3. A 'clockwork' universe of the Laplacean type—that is, one governed by strictly deterministic laws.

Mediation. The process of connecting two end terms by an intermediary. In logic, mediate inference connects the major and minor terms by means of the middle term. In Neoplatonism, God and the world are related by mediation. In theology, Christ is the mediator between God and the world.

Meditation. The act of concentrating attention on God or self to increase one's insight about, or relation, to spiritual things.

Megarian School. A philosophical school active at Megara, near Athens, between the late 5th and early 3rd centuries BC. No writings of the Megarians have survived and our knowledge of their doctrines and interests is based on references in the works of their contemporaries. They were influenced by Socrates and the Eleatics and were critical of Plato and Aristotle. Some of their contributions to logic are of lasting interest. Eubulides, the refiner of the liar paradox, was one of their number.

Meliorism. From the Latin melior meaning 'butter'. The doctrine that man, while incapable of perfection, is capable of an indefinitely extending series of improvements. This applies both to the individual man and to the race.

Memory. The capacity to bring to mind (a) an event from one's past experience ('I remember my first day at school') or (b) a previously learnt truth ('I remember the formula for this', 'I remember that the book was removed from the shelf'). It is commonly agreed, however, that memory is closely related to knowledge, either as a special case of knowledge, or in so far as it is only possible to remember what was once knon.

A central problem about memory concerns how it is possible to acquire present knowledge of that which is no longer present.

Mentalism. Any doctrine insisting upon the exclusive reality of minds and their inner states; the them is also applied to those views of mind which distinguish mental states from brain states.

Mentality. The quality of mind is treated under such topics as 'idealism' and 'soul.' But Morgan held mentality to be the emergent of the psychical correlate. And Whitehead regarded the 'mental pole' as originative of novelty in the universe.

Meta. Originally a Greek preposition, now employed by English-speakng philosophers as a prefix. The usual meaning is 'about as in 'meta-ethics', 'metahistory', and 'metalanguage'.

Metahistory. In the broad sense, philosopy of history. The term is often resticted to the discipline's speculative aspect, which attempts to establish a framework of principles that can account for the course of historical developments.

Metalanguage. The language used to talk about an object language and its component words.

Metalogic. The term refers simply to the metalanguage of logic. It is a study of the structure, signs connectives, formulae, theorems, and rules of inference of logic from a syntactic, semantic, and pragmatic point of view. The basic concepts, upon which discussion of metalogic has turned in recent years, are decidability completeness, and consistency.

Metamathematics. The study of formal systems, and, especially, of the concepts used in mathematics. It is also called proof theory.

Metaphilosophy. In terms of subject-matter, Metaphilosophy is the discussion of the nature of philosophy, including of course the nature of its constituent disciplines of Logic, Ethics, Aesthetics, Epistemology, etc.

Metaphysics. A central element in Western philosophy from the Greeks onwards, 'metaphysics' has meant many different things. It can be an attempt to characterize existence or reality as a whole, instead of, as in the various natural sciences, particular parts or aspects thereof. Materialism and idealism, Spinoza's monism and Leibniz's monadology, are examples of metaphysics in this sense. It can also be an attempt to explore the realm of the suprasensible, beyond the world of experience; to establish indubitable first principles as a foundation for all other knowledge; to examine critically what more limited studies simply take for granted; or to compile an inventory of what sorts of things ultimately, or in the last analysis, there are.

Metempsychosis. The idea, found in Buddhism and other religions originating in the Indian subcontinent, that our souls have lived before in the bodies of other men or of non-human animals, and that after death they will in due course be reincarnated into other human or non-human bodies.

Methodological Holism and Methodological Individualism. Rival banners in an imbroglio in the philosophy of social science. One side presses for explanation in terms of social structures and social wholes, the other insists that everything must be reduced to statements about the component individuals.

Methodology. Refers to the study of method, usually covering the procedures and aims of a particular discipline, and enquiry into the way in which that discipline is organized.

Middle Platonism. The developments in Platonism that took place between the establishing of the so-called Middle Academy by Arcesilaus and the advent of Plotinus.

Milesian (or Ionian) School. The group of Presocratics who came from the then Greek cities of the Aegean coast of what is now Turkey. The known figures are Thales, Anaximander, and Anaximenes (all form Miletus), and Anaxagoras of Clazomenae (who spent all his working life in Athens until he was expelled, nominally for godlessness). According to this, 'the earth is full of gods' expresses this conviction that all forces are forces of the Universe itself.

Millet Seed Paradox. A puzzle, also known as the heap, and arises out of the attack on plurality and on the evidence of the senses by Zeno of Elea.

Mill's Methods. The four 'methods of experimental inquiry' distinguished by J.S. Mill his in Logic (III) (viii). Mill held that all induction involves a search for causes and the methods are thus also contributions to the definition of 'cause'.

Mimamsa. One of the systems of Indian philosophy. Originally it concerned itself solely with the hermeneutics of the ancient ritualistic scriptures; this discipline was systematized by Jaimini in the Karma-mimamsasutras (before the 2nd century AD).

Mimesis. A Greek term meaning 'imitation.' When Plato held that 'time is the moving image of eternity,' he was saying that the world is an image or an imitation of the eternal forms or ideas.

Mind-body Problem. The philosophical problem of how the mind is related to the body, and of what properties, functions, and occurrences should be regarded as, respectively, mental or physical. This problem is central to both the philosophy of mind and the philosophy of psychology.

Mind, Philosophy, of. The philosophical study of the mind and mental functioning. While the principal task of the philosophy of mind may be regarded as the attempt to provide an account of what mind is, the complexity of the task is such that there is little in philosophical literature that will seem to constitute an integrated theory of the mind per se. Rather, issues that are central to the philosophy of mind occur throughout metaphysics, epistemology, logic, aesthetics, and, particularly, in the contexts of the philosophy of psychology and what is called the mind-body problem.

Minor Premises. In a categorical syllogism, the premise having the minor term.

Minor Term. The subject term of the conclusion of a categorical syllogism.

Miracle. A term that is most commonly taken to mean an act that manifests divine power through the suspension or alteration of the normal working of the laws of nature. The idea of laws of nature is thus essential to the idea of the miraculous, but is also, clearly, a major barrier to belief that miracles actually occur.

Modality. Refers to the way in which a sentence may characterize another related sentence or proposition as true, that is, the mode in which it is true.

Modal Logic. The logic of necessity and possibility. A modal statement is one in which something is said to be necessarily, or possibly the case.

Mode. From the Latin modus meaning 'manner'. In philosophy the term refers to the manner of existence of a thing or substance.

Model

1. (of a set of sentences) An interpretation (usually a set-theoretic interpretation) of the language in which the sentences are written, which assigns to each sentence of the set the value 'true'.

2. (of a formal system) An interpretation of the set of axioms of that system.

Model Theory. A branch of mathematical logic devoted to the study of logical relations and of the properties of formal system via their models, that is, set-theoretic interpretations.

Modernism. Although the term suggests that any one who takes the norms of modern thought and life as decisive in his interpretation of the matter would be a modernist and believe is in modernism, the term in fact has an almost exclusive reference to religious thought.

Modus. Latin term meaning 'mode'. Used by the Scholastics in relation to modal propositions.

Modus Ponens. (Latin for : mood that affirms.) In its basic form, an argument that runs 'If *p*, then *q*.*p*. Therefore *q* Affirming the antecedent.

Modus Tollens. (Latin for : mood that denies.) In its basic form, an argument that runs 'If *p*, then *q*. But not-*q*. Therefore not-*p*.' Affirming the antecedent.

Mohammedanism. The religion founded by Mohammed. The faith is characterized by an exclusive monotheism, the worship of Allah as the one true God, and Mohammed as the greatest of his prophets.

Moism. Chinese philosophical movement, resting on the doctrine of universal love, and providing the chief alternative to Confucianism between the 5th and 3rd centuries B.C.

Moksa. (Sanskrit for : liberation.) In most systems of Indian thought, final release from the cycle of rebirth (samsara) and the sorrows and preplexities of the material world. In this eternal repose the soul recovers its innate integrity; how this is thought to be achieved—whether by merging with brahman or by eternal existence as a pure spirit—differs from system to system. Only the heretical materialists denied the doctrine, together with the related doctrines of samsara and karma. Compare nirvana.

Monad. From the Greek term monas meaning 'unit'.

The term's first use was in Pythagorean number theory where it was the name of the first number of the series, and thus the number from which all other numbers were derived.

Giordano Bruno used the term as the name of the irreducible ontological unit of which all else in made up.

Monadic. In logic denoting a predicate that requires only the addition of one singular term is order to make a well formed sentence... '...flies' and... '...is large' are monadic (or oneplace) predicates.

Monadology. The title given by one of Leibniz's editors to a metaphysical work written by Leibniz in 1714, and now applied to any metaphysical system such as Leibniz's.

Monarchy. From the Greek monos ('alone') and archein ('to be first'). A form of government characterized by the rule of one person.

Monasticism. From the Greek monazein ('to be alone'). A discipline of life characterized by withdrawal from the world, meditation, self-abnegation and some degree of asceticism.

Monism. A philosophical theory that maintains that there is one, and only one, substance. Examples of this type of theory are provided by the philosophies of Spinoza and Hegel.

Mood. One of the various ways in which (valid) syllogisms may be constructed within the four figures of the categorical syllogism. The valid syllogism in each figure are called the moods of that figure.

Moral. Opposed to immoral.

Moral Argument for the Existence of God. An argument best known in the formulation by Kant, which attempts to find sufficient grounds for theism in the specifically moral experience of mankind. According to the Kantian form of the argument, the highest good is a state of affairs in which happiness is distributed in strict proportion to moral virtue.

Morality. In many usages, a synonym of the term, 'ethics' (where most of the issues common to both terms are treated).

Shaftesbury held morality to be natural, and independent of supernatural sanctions.

Moral Sense. A supposed faculty for detecting moral properties. Moral sense theory, a form of intiutionism popular in the 18th century, holds that the perception of certain actions (or events) arouses distinctive feelings of pleasure or pain in the spectator. These feelings serve both to enable him to distinguish right actions from wrong, and to provide motives to moral behaviour.

Moral Sense Theory. The ethical theory that we are able to distinguish between right and wrong by a distinctive moral sense.

Mortalist. Refers to a person who believes that when people die that is that, and there is no survival.

Moslem. From the Arabic muslim ('one who submits'). One who professes the faith of Islam, *i.e.*, a follower of Mohammed.

Motion. Change in the relative positions of bodies.

Paramenides, Zeno, and Nagarjuna argued against the possibility of motion.

Music of the Spheres. The superb music believed by Pythagoreans to be produced by the regular movements of the heavenly bodies. No earthy ears—except perhaps those of Pythagoras himself—have had the good fortune to hear it.

Mystery Religions. The name given to a group of religous cults popular in the Hellenic and Roman periods. The mystery religions were characterized by a body of esoteric knowledge and ceremony which allegedly had the power to purify the initiate and guarantee him union with God and personal immortality. Virtually all of the mysteries centered around dying and rising saviors.

Mysticism. What is claimed to be direct or unmediated experience of the divine, in which the human soul momentarily approaches union with God. Many of the great mystics have stressed that this is not primarily or essentially a matter of visions or ecstasies, as is sometimes supposed, but of total submission of the human will and intellect to God.

Myth. From the Greek term mythos meaning 'legend.' Hence, a narrative account taken to be true, but not known to be true. The elaboration of dramatic narratives involving superhuman powers provided the first explanations of the origin and operation of the universe. Myth has some relation to metaphor and can be treated as allegory.

Myth of Er. The concluding parable in Plato's Republic (Book X) concerning the fate of souls after death and the choices available to them before reincarnation. The warrior, Er, apparently slain in battle, returns to the world to narrate his vision of the after-life, in which the pursuit of wisdom and justice is shown to be the soul's only safeguard against present folly and future degradation. It is noteworthy that Plato, having insisted in the Republic, as elsewhere, that the soul is essentially incorporeal, is quite unable, and makes no attempt, to describe the doings and sufferings of supposedly disembodied souls in any terms other than those appropriate to flesh and blood persons.

N

Nagarjuna. 100-200. Indian philosopher. A Buddhist and the first systematic expounder of an important school, called Shunyavada holding to the relativity of thought, and the non-duality of the Absolute. The school is also known as the Madhyamika or Doctrine school. There are two aspects to his thought, one negative and the other positive.

Principle writings : Twenty Verses on the Great Vehicle (T); Treatise on the Middle Doctrine (T); Treatise on Relativity (T).

Naive Realism. The perfectly gratuitous view that all of the qualities we sense in objects—including sounds, colors, tastes, smells, and tactile sensations, as well as shapes and motions—are in fact characteristics of these objects.

Nanak. Founder of the Sikh religion.

Nastika. Sanskrit term which means 'denier.' It applies to any Indian system of thought not accepting the authority of the Vedas. Examples are Charvaka, and Buddhism. To be contrasted with the Astika systems which accept the Vedas as authoritative.

Natural Deduction System. Refers to a set of rules for the construction of deductive arguments without any axioms or postulates.

Naturalism. This term refers to the philosophical belief that what is studied by the non-human and human sciences is all there is, and the denial of the need for any explanation going beyond or outside the Universe.

Naturalistic Fallacy. The mistake (which it is not universally agreed always is a mistake) of deducing conclusions about what ought to be from premises that state only what is the case; or the other way about. This was first labelled by G.E. Moore in Principia Ethica (1903).

Natural Language. An ordinary language, such as English, Russian, or Chinese, contrasted either with an artificial language such as Esperanto or Ido, or with a formal language which may be no more than an uninterpreted logical calculus.

Natural Theology. The attempt to prove the existence of God, and sometimes human immortality too, from premises provided by observation of the ordinary course of nature.

Natural Rights. The rights which belong to man by nature, resting not an custom or convention, but on self-evident principles or fundamental laws of reason.

Natural Theology. Any theology which purports to rest its case on reason instead of revelation.

Natura Naturans and Natura Naturata. Latin phrases meaning 'nature naturing' and 'nature natured,' respectively. 'Nature naturing' applies to God as the creative principle of created things, or infinite and eternal Being over against finite, temporal beings. 'Nature natured' applies to the created things which find their principle in God.

Nature. From the Latin natura, a translation of the Greek word physis. Both terms derive from roots suggesting production, growth, and bringing to birth. Thus the early signification of the term concerned that part of reality subject to change; and physics was the name of the study charged with the understanding of this aspect of reality.

Naya. A Sanskrit term which means 'aspect or standpoint.' In Jainism there are seven nayas from which one can view reality.

Necessary and Contingent Truth. A proposition is said to be necessarily true, or to express a logically necessary truth, iff the denial of that proposition would involve a self-contradiction; a proposition which happens to be contingently true, or to express a logically contingent truth, is one which could nevertheless be denied, or asserted, without self-contradiction.

Necessary and Sufficient Conditions. This is a necessary condition for that iff that cannot be without this. This is a sufficient condition for that iff this is by itself enough to guarantee that. Necessary and sufficient conditions may both be either logically necessary or logically contingent.

Necessitarianism. Refers to the doctrine that all events happen by necessity, having either logical or causal determination, and that the will is not free. A synonym for 'determinism'.

Necessity. From the Latin ne ('not') plus cedere ('to go away'). The Greek term is anagke, and the original concept probably concerned fate or destiny. Necessity may be affirmed of propositions, of things, or of God.

When affirmed of propositions, to say that a proposition is necessary is to say that it is not possible to deny that proposition.

Negation From the Latin term nego, meaning 'deny.' In philosophy the term applies to the denial of a class or property, statement or proposition.

Neo-Confucianism. (Chinese tao hsueh : the learning of the Way.) A vague term often applied to all developments in Confucianism from the Sung revival in the 11th century onward. This began as a deliberate effort to restore Confucian authority over a society in which, since the 5th century, Buddhism had become entrenched at every level.

Neo-Kantianism. An umbrella term for several philosophical movements in Germany between about 1870 and 1920, often very disparate but all tracing their inspiration back to the spirit, critical method, and works of Kant. They diverged over the emphasis that they placed on different parts of Kant's work, but shared a reaction against speculative metaphysics and a return to the Kantian intention of a synthesis of empiricism and rationalism. Six different (and often opposing) schools are usually distinguished, perhaps the most influential being the Marburg school.

Neoplatonism. One of the most persistent strands of Western philosophy, Neoplatonism is, as the name suggests, a philosophy which begins from the work of Plato, and interprets him in a special manner. The manner of that interpretation tends to associate God with the principle of unity, making Him completely transcendent, and related to the world by means of a series of intermediaries, who (or which) derive from the One by a principle of emanation. In this view reality is a graded series from the divine to the material, and man, who has in him some part of the divine, longs for union with the eternal source of things. The system thus has spiritual as well as intellectual implications.

Neopythagoreanism. A movement, originating in the 1st century BC, the main tenets of which were a blend of the teachings of Pythagoras with Platonic, Stoic, and Peripatetic material. Mysticism, number symbolism, and astrology were characteristic of Neopythagorean thought, and it was an important precursor of Neoplatonism.

Neo-Taoism. (Chinese hsueh : mysterious learning.) An eclectic form of Taoism that flourished in China c. 225-375 A.D. Its exponents used the Lao-tzu, Chuang-tzu, and I-ching (Book of Changes) as a basis for discussing problems such as the relation between being and non-being, and the nature of absolute knowledge and communication.

Neo-Thomism. The movement reviving the actual or supposed ideas of St. Thomas Aquinas.

Nestorianism. A Christological doctrine of the 5th century A.D. advanced by Nestorius, Patriarch of Constantinople. Terming it a 'prosopic union' of the divine and human (from the Greek term prosopon meaning 'face'), Nestorius held 'the manhood is the face of the God head, and the Godhead is the face of the manhood'. This was misinterpreted as the doctrine that the God man is two complete persons. It is this misinterpretation that bears the name, Nestorian heresy.

Neti Neti. Sanskrit phrase which means 'Not this, not this.' Employed in the Brhadaranyaka Upanishad, and by shankara as the only appropriate definition of Brahman.

Neutral Monism. The doctrine that the basic entities of the world are neither physical nor mental, but of some neutral 'stuff' which, organized in one manner, yields physical entities, or bodies, and, when organized in another manner, yields mind. The doctrine was held.

New Philosophers, the A group of French social philosophers, coming into prominence in the 1970's Anti-establishment. anti-Marxist, and anti-ideological, they are the fruit of the May, 1968, student and worker uprising. Among 1444; Apology for Learned Ignorance, 1449; The Idiot, 14:0; The Vision of God. 1453; On the Peace of Faith, 1453; as well as mathematical treatises.

Neustic. See phrastic and neustic.

Neutral Monism. See monism.

Newton, Isaac (1642-1727). British mathematician and physicit who formalized Galilean mechanics, discovered the inverse square law of universal gravitation, and made notable contributions to the theory of light.

Nihilism. From the Latin nihil ('nothing'). A doctrine denying validity to any positive alternative, the term has been applied to metaphysics, epistemology, ethics, politics, and theology. The term was coined by Turgeniev in his novel Fathers and Children (1862) to apply to a Russian movement is the second half to the 19th century which pressed for change without a plan and which at its height, assassinated numbers of Russian officials including the Tsar Alexander II himself.

Nirguna Brahman. From the Sanskrit nir ('without') plus guna ('attributes'). Hence, that from of Brahman without attributes or qualities.

Nirvana. Sanskrit term which means 'blown out,' referring to the extinction of all worldly desires. Referring to the state of release, or salvation, the term is most often associated with Buddhism.

Nisus. A Latin term which means 'striving.'

Niyama. The second step of Yogic meditation, that of positive ethical preparation.

Noble Savage. The romantic conception of man as enjoying a natural and noble existence until civilization makes him a slave to unnatural wants and seduces him from his original freedom.

Noetic. 1. In general, cognitive. **2.** In contrast to empirical and sensuous, pertaining to that which can be apprehended by reason alone.

Nomic. Pertaining to a law (of nature).

Nominalism. (In scholastic philosophy) The view that universals have no existence independently of being thought and are mere names, representing nothing that really exists. The nominalist thus denies anything like Plato's theory of Forms or Ideas.

Nomothetic. Proposing or prescribing a law (of nature).

Noncontradiction, Principle of. Probably the better name for that one of the three laws of thought usually called the Principle of Contradiction. If we accept as its standard statement, 'It is not the case that p is true and not-p is true,' the principle urges upon us the avoidance of contradiction, and hence the appropriateness of the above name.

Non-Euclidean Geometry. A geometry that denies the parallel postulate of Euclid. Euclid's Elements provides the postulates from which all the theorems of classical (or Euclidean) geometry may be deduced. A version of Euclid's fifth postulate (the parallel postulate) is that, given a straight line and a point not on this line, there exists exactly one straight line through the point parallel to the first line. One may insist, as Lobachevsky did, that there are many parallel lines, or, with Riemann, that there are no parallel lines. The simplest statement of Einstein's theory of relativity uses Riemannian geometry.

Non Sequitur. Latin phrase meaning 'it does not follow.' In logic, a conclusion that does not follow from its premises.

No-ownership Theory. A metaphysical doctrine of the self, labelled by Strawson. It arises from Cartesian mind-body dualism and maintains that conscious experiences associated wite a subject cannot be said to 'belong' to that consciousness : 'Only those things whose ownership is logically transferable can be owned at all.'

Normal Form. A notion that plays an important role in proof theory. In trying to prove a result about a language L in which proofs can be constructed according to stipulated rules of inference, it is useful to know that, or whether, all propositions expressible in the language can be expressed in some standard (or normal) form.

Normative. Tending to establish a standard of correctness by prescription of rules; evaluative rather than descriptive.

Normative Ethics. The traditional view of Ethics that it is part of the task of the moral philosopher to provide guidance with respect to issues of right and wrong, good and evil. Normative ethics is to be distinguished from Meta. Ethics, the analysis of the logic of ethics and the systems of those who treat of Normative Ethics.

Nothing. The term is a synonym for the philosophical term, 'non-being,' and is thus the formal complement to the term, 'being'. The fact of this complementarity has led even those who wish to grant reality only to various kinds of being, to make reference to non-being, or nothing.

No-true-scotsman Move. The term used for a nickname for a manoeuvre that meets the falsification of some cherished generalization by maintaining that the predicate in question, while not perhaps applicable to all run of the mill so-and-sos, is nevertheless essential to true so-and sos.

Noumenon. From the Greek noumenon which means equally 'thing perceived' and 'what is known.' Plato used the term occasionally and always in the latter sense, to refer to the intelligibles or 'things of thought.'

Nous. (Greek for : mind.) A term used by the Presocratics to indicate knowledge and reason. For Plato is meant the rational part of the soul. For Aristotle it was the intellect, in which he distinguished between active and passive reason, the former alone being immortal and eternal.

Null (or Empty) Set. The set with no members. It is usually symbolized as ϕ.

Number. Beginning with the Pythagorean insight that reality is to be understood in terms of numerical expressions the status of number and the nature of numerical entities have occupied philosophers no less than have the status and nature of ideas. Indeed, the basic positions of Realism. Conceptualism, and Nominalism, which appear in the discussions of Universals reappear in the corresponding discussions of number. In these discussions, however, the terms favored for the respective positions are Platonism, Intuitionism, and Nominalism.

Nyaya. One of the six systems of Indian thought to arise in the period following the Vedic Age, and the formation of the Bhagavad-Gita and many of the sutras. The system was founded by a man named Gautama It shares with the Vaisesika system a metaphysics which endorses atomistic pluralism and logical realism. But while Vaisesika stresses the metaphysicaland ontological side of things, Nyaya is directed toward consideration of logical and epistemological problems. Nyaya provided the logic, as it were, for the other systems.

O

Object. From the Latin ob ('over against') and jacere ('to throw'). The ordinary current meaning of object is that which exists in its own right, as a thing outside the mind. But, initially, that was the meaning of the word 'subject'. When the term came into philosophy use in the Middle Ages the widely held meaning of object (or objectum) was whatever is designated by any intentions reference.

Object Language

1. (relative to a metalanguage) A language discussed in a metalanguage. Such a language may itself be a metalanguage relative to some third language.

2 (absolute) A language used to talk only about non-linguistic subjects, such as physical objects of numbers.

Obligation From the Latin obligare (from ob, 'to', and ligare, 'to bind'). One important tradition in ethics centers on the ideas of obligation and duty. The theory of obligation is called deontology from the Greek deon ('obligation'). Deontic logic studies the types of necessity present in statements of obligation.

Obverse Immediate Inference (3).

Obversion. Immediate Inference (3).

Obvertend. Immediate Inference (3).

Obligation. Refers to a duty that a person is under a moral compulsion to perform if he has a role in society and there are moral rules in that society dictating that anyone playing this role must thereby perform that act. Thus a father has obligations, qua father, to his children, a promiser, qua promiser, to the promisee, etc. Not all duties or obligations are voluntarily self-imposed. A citizen may have obligations to the state even though that role was not one which he chose to adopt.

Obverse Refers to the statement which is derived by obversion of the original and logically equivalent to it. Obversion of a categorical statement is performed by negating the predicate term and changing the statement from negative ro affirmative, or vice versa.

Obversion. In scholastic logic, a form of immediate inference. Aristotle did not regard it as a valid form of inference.

Occasionalism. A doctrine which was put forward by Malebranche. This doctrine attempts to plug a notorious gap in Cartesian thinking on the mind-body problem. How can mind and body, supposed to be two radically distinct substances, causally interact ? The occasionalists baldly deny and such interaction to be possible : the will of man is incapable of moving the smallest body. How then does my arm go up when I will it ?

The true cause, claim the occasionalists, is divine intervention, my willing being merely the occasion for that intervention.

Ockhamism. The term used for the movement of thought initiated by William of Ockham. It consisted in criticism of Scholasticism, an emphasis on empirical method, and a heightened appreciation of the role of religious faith

Ockham's Razor. The principle of ontological economy, usually formulated as 'Entities are not to be multiplied beyond necessity. These actual words are not in fact to be found in the extant works of William of Ockham.

Oedipus Effect. Refers to the impact of the making of a statement, in particular a predictive statement, upon the human situation to which that statement refers.

Oligarchy From the Greek oligoi ('few') and arche ('rule') The term literally signifies a form of government characterized by minority rule. For Plato and Aristotle, however, it stood for that form of government where the wealthy few rule for their own interests.

Om. A Sanskrit term connoting assent. Originally, aum, the three letters respectively standing for the absolute, the relative, and the relation between them. Now the mystic and sacred syllable of Hinduism, identified in the Isa, Mundaka, Mandukya, Taittiriya, and Chandogya Upanishads as standing for the whole world and its parts, including past, present, and future, as well as for Atman, the self of all things. Pronunciation of the syllable in religious devotion and meditation is a feature of many Indian-based systems.

Omnipotence. From the Latin omnis ('all') and potens ('powerful'). One of the chief attributes of the absolutistic conception of God. That view should be compared with others in which God is regarded as finite in some respects and infinite in other respects. Nor is the conception of God as a finite being negligible in Western thought.

Omnipresence One of the traditional attributes of God. If a thing or being is where it works, then the problem of the divine omni!t presence becomes part of the problem of omnipotence and -he distinctions important to that concept likewise apply here.

Omniscience From the Latin omnis ('all') and scire ('to know). Traditionally, one of the chief attributes of God.

In traditional theology the attribute of omniscience includes completely detailed knowledge of the future as well as knowledge of the past and present.

Omniscience, Paradoxes of. Problems arising over how God's omniscience can be consistent with his timelessness on his granting freewill to mankind, given that omniscience includes fore-knowledge of future events (including human actions).

One. From the Latin unus and the Greek oine. In Pythagorean number theory the 'One' and the 'Dyad' generate all other numbers.

For Plato the One interpenetrates with Beauty, Truth, and the Good to make something close to a single eternal principle.

One-many Problem. Refers to the problem of how we should account for the fact that we can correctly apply one and the same word to many distinct things.

Ontological Argument. An argument for God which moves from the definition of His nature as a perfect being to the conclusion that He exists. The argument has several versions.

Ontology. From the Greek ontos ('being') and logos ('knowledge'). The term thus means 'knowledge of being' and refers to a division of philosophy having such knowledge as its subject matter.

Ontology. Refers to the branch of metaphysical enquiry which is concerned with the study of existence itself (considered apart from the nature of any existent object) It differentiates between 'real existence' and 'appearance' and investigates the different ways in which entities belonging to various logical categories (physical objects, numbers, universals, abstractions, etc.) may be said to exist.

Open Society. A society structured to allow its members to advance to whatever level their capacities allow.

Open Question Argument. A test which was introducing by G. E. Moore, for demonstrating the failure of any proposed definition of 'good'. If 'X is Y' is a definition, then the question 'Is YX ?' cannot be substantial or, as some say, 'open'. But all questions of the form 'Is Y good?' are. Moore claims, 'open' in this sense; therefore 'good' is indefinable.

Open Texture. The expression introduced in an influential 1945 article by Friedrich Waismann as a translation of his original German coinage Porositat der Begriffe. It is not, he explained, to be confused with vagueness, being rather the possibility of vagueness. It characterizes most though not all empirical concepts.

Operation. A one-place operation is a function of one argument whose range is included in its domain.

Operationalism. A philosophical position first announced by the physicist, P. W. Bridgman, to the effect that scientific concepts are to be defined in terms of operations; and the meanings of such concepts are identical to the operations entering into their definitions. His standard example was the manner in which a given length is identical to a set of measuring operations with a ruler. Under pressure, he added pencil and paper operations to allow more abstract definitions. Hugo Dingler independently developed a similar approach.

Operator. Refers to the which effects an operation. In logic it is usually expressed as a symbol. Corresponding to each function on objects there is a symbolic operation effected by the symbol for that function.

Opinion Parmenides contrasted opinion with truth, the former relating to sense experience and dealing with appearance, the latter relating to thought and dealing with reality and being.

Optimism and Pessimism. Contrasting attitudes concerning the predominace of good or evil in the world. The former represents general hopefulness regarding the balance of pleasure and pain; the latter the view that hope is unreasonable and that happiness, if attainable, lies beyond the sphere of ordinary experience. The prevailing tone of a particular philosophical system depends mainly upon that system's cosmology and its account of man's role in the Universe.

Oracles, Chaldean. A philosophical poem of the 2nd century A.D. describing the descent of the soul into the realm of matter and its possible rise after purification, through the concentric circles of the universe toward its eterm home. Containing Platonic.

Order. An arrangement in accordance with intention, principle, or rule

According to Hesig order came out of chaos through the power of Eros. In addition to eros Greek philosophy has explored many other possible ordering principles, including mind and chance variation.

Both linear and hierarchical order are implicit in Plato's notion that the world of change has as its pattern a world of ideas. The possibility of graded order is likewise present in medieval thought where the idea of order depends upon a relation of adequation or commensurability between a thing and its idea in the mind of God.

Ordered Pair. A pair the basic property of which is that two pairs are identical iff the first members of each are identical and the second members of each are identical.

Order Type. The set of all sets ordinally similar to a given set.

Ordinary Languge. Ordinary (for example, non-technical and plain) language contrasts with esoteric (for example, technical or jargon). Note however, the difference between 'the use of ordinary language' and 'the ordinary use of "..."' 'Ordinary use' means 'standard use' and even specialist words may have standard uses.

Organism, Philosophy of. Just as some philosophers have taken matter and mind as the key to metaphysics others have found the key in the concept of 'organism.' The philosophy of organism, sometimes called 'organicism,' is the result.

Organismic Biology. The name of that interpretation of biology which stresses the non-reductionistic nature of the organic level, taking the position that the whole cannot be equated simply with the sum of the activities of the parts.

Organon. (Greek for : instrument, tool (Latin Organum)) The name traditionally given to Aristotle's six treatises on logic : Categories; De Interpretation; Prior Analytics; Posterior Analytics Topics; and Sophistical Refutations.

Original Sin. In traditional Christain teaching, the doctrine that the whole human race inherits, and is corrupted by, the sinfulness first brought into the world through the disobedience of Adam and Eve. Hence, since the Fall, human nature as such has been inherently sinful, a state from which it can be rescued only by divine grace.

Orphism. A modern term for two related but different phenomena of ancient Greek religion.

1. A massive tradition of writing, beginning as early as the 7th century BC and supposedly inspired, if not composed, by the mythical singer Orpheus.
2. The way of life expected of those initiated into the Mysteries of Eleusis.

Orthodoxy. From the Greek orthos ('right') and doxa ('opinion'). Correctness of belief as determined by an authoritative standard. To be contrasted with heterodoxy or heresy.

Othering. Plato's concept of negation.

Other Minds. The problem whether and how anyone knows that any other organism is sentient. For, surely, there is no contradiction in suggesting that the behaviour and talk of others might in every way resemble mine though they were unconscious automata; while someone in a cataleptic trance might be to all appearance dead, yet conscious.

Ousia. A Greek term meaning 'being,' 'substance,' or 'essence.'

Aristotle used the term to refer primarily to the individual, existing thing. This he called ousia prote or 'first substance'.

P

Panentheism. From the Greek pan and theos meaning 'all in God.' The view that all reality is part of the being of God. To be distinguished from Pantheism which identifies God with the total reality.

Panpsychism. The theory that holds that the world is rendered more comprehensible on the assumption that every object is invested with a soul or mind.

Pansomatism. The doctrine of Kotarbinski that every sentient entity is a body.

Pantheism. Refers to the doctrine that the divine is all-inclusive and that man and Nature are not independent of God, but are modes or elements of his Being. Its precisé significance—if such indeed there is—depends on the initial conceptions of God (and independence).

Paraclete. From the Greek parakaleo ('to call to one'). Hence, a witness, advocate, helper, or comforter. The term is usually applied to the role of the Holy Spirit.

Paradigm. In the philosophy of science, a central overall way of regarding phenomena, within which a scientist normally works.

Paradigm Case Argument Refers to the argument that infers from the fact that a word is taught by reference to clear (paradigm) cases, the conclusion that examples of the thing referred to by the word must exist.

Paradox. A situation arising when, from a number of premises all generally accepted as true, a conclusion is reached by valid deductive argument that is either an outright contradiction or conflicts with other generally held beliefs.

Parallelism, Psychophysical. The doctrine that there is a one-to-one correspondence of physical and psychical events throughout the universe.

Paralogism. From the Greek para ('beside') and logos ('reason'). Thus, the idea of a conclusion which does not follow reason, *i.e.* a fallacious syllogism.

Pascal's Wager. An argument known chiefly from its formulation by Pascal in his posthumous Pensees, but certainly developed earlier.

Passion. From the Latin passio, a translation of the Greek pathos ('a passive condition').

One of the categories of Aristotle passion contrasts with action and refers to the condition of a thing as acted upon by other things. The passion of a thing thus refers not to the essence but to the accidents of things, and has a passive sense.

Past, the. One of the modes of time, the concept of the past has not received a great deal of attention in terms of philosophical analysis.

Bergson presented a doctrine of the past as internal to the present. His analogy is that of a rolling snowball containing its earlier states.

Patanjali. 2nd-century B.C. Indian philosopher. Founder of the Yoga system. He held Yoga to be a method of attaining salvation through the control of the physical and psychical features of human nature.

Principal writings : Yoga Sutra.

Pathetic Fallacy. The accepted name for the mistake—not strictly a fallacy—of attributing to inanimate objects the feelings, dispositions, and reactions which could only characterize animate creatures, and in particular people.

Patristics. From the Latin pater ('father'). The term refers to the Church Fathers and their works in the period between the end of the New Testament period, and the beginnings of Scholasticism with Erigena in the 9th century.

Peano's Postulates. Five postulates (or axioms) from which the rest of arithmetic can be developed. They were presented by Giuseppe Peano in 1889 (although Richard Dedekind had in fact published them previously in 1888) in order to free the concept of number from dependence upon mere institution. They are :

(1) 0 is a number.

(2) The successor of any number is a number.

(3) No two numbers have the same successor.

(4) 0 is not the successor of any number.

(5) If P is a predicate true of 0, and if whenever P is true of a number n it is also true of the successor of n, then P is true of every number.

Pelagianism. A heresy, propagated by the 5th-century British monk Pelagius. It denied original sin and held that man can, of his own freewill and without the intervention of God's grace, live sinless and attain eternal life.

Perception. From the Latin percipio, which covers both the obtaining of knowledge through the senses, and apprehension with the mind.

Perfection. From the Latin perfectio meaning 'completeness' or 'completion'. The concept has been applied primarily to God, and then in a derivative sense to man.

Perfection, Principle of. A principle of the philosophy of Leibniz, which states that God creates the best of all possible worlds, that is, a world in which a maximum of perfection is achieved with a minimum of deficiency.

Per Genus et Differentiam. (Latin for : by kind and difference.) A method of definition characteristic of Aristotelian logic.

Peripatetic. A follower of Aristotle, the word deriving from restless practices in his Lyceum.

Perlocution. An utterance with perlocutionary effects. Effects that may (but need not) by caused by utterances (for example, embarrassment) are called their 'perlocutionary effects'.

Person. From the Latin persona, a translation of the Greek prosopon, both words signifying the mask worn by actors onstage.

By extension the reference is to the role an individual plays in the drama of life.

Personal Identity. The concept posing the philosophical problem of explaining what it means to say that this at this time is the same person as that at that time.

Personalism. The theory, largely of 20th-century American origin, that the person is ontologically fundamental, and that all philosophical enquiry should proceed in reference to the concept of person.

Personalism. A philosophical position taking the concept of 'person' as ultimate.

Perspectivism. Refers to the view that the external world is to be interpreted through different alternative systems of concepts and beliefs and that there is no authoritative independent criterion for determining that one such system is more valid than another.

Phenomenalism. From the Greek phainomenon ('appearance'). The view that we know only phenomena, and that there are no things behind phenomena causing their appearance. When one separates the phenomena of which one is aware from the objects causing one to have this awareness, the problem arises of determining what these causative objects may be. The difficulties present in the dualism of phenomenon and object have led a number of philosophers to the position of phenomenalism.

Phenomenology. From the Greek phainomenon ('appearance') and logos ('knowledge of'). In general, phenomenology is an approach to philosophy centering on analysis of the phenomena which flood man's awareness.

Phenomenon. Any object or occurrence perceived by the senses.

1. (in Greek philosophy) Sensible appearance, contrasted with the real object apprehended by the intellect.

2. (in Kant) The object interpreted through categories, contrasted with noumenon.

Philosopheme. From the Greek philosophema referring to a philosophical proposition or demonstration. Aristotle used the term to distinguish demonstrative reasoning from rhetoric, eristic, and dialectic.

Philosopher Kings. In Plato's Republic, genuine rulers and philosophers who, knowing the Platonic Forms or Ideas, thus become experts about ends and values.

Philosopher's Stone The hypothetical substance sought by alchemists (alchemy) for converting base metals into gold. It appears in the alchemical literature under hundreds of different and fanciful names.

Philosophes

1. The designation of fashionable and influential thinkers of the Enlightenment.

2. In the Encyclopedie, one of the areas of the literary world (contrasted with erudites and beaux esprits) : the field of wisdom distinguished from the field of learning and pleasure.

Philosophical Radicals. Followers of Bentham, themselves primarily theoreticians, who aimed at and achieved considerable practical influence.

Philosophy. Most of what might have appeared here as a general description of what philosophy is about will instead be found in the Preface. There are text articles on the various branches of philosophy : aesthetics, ethics, epistemology, logic, and metaphysics. Articles will also be found on the philosophies of education, history, language, law, mind, psychology, religion, science, and space and time, and on political and social philosophy.

Philosophy of Science. A discipline which attempts to relate philosophy to the fields of scientific inquiry. Depending upon the orientation of the philosopher and the area of science, the goal of philosophy of science is to discover the nature of science, of the nature of scientific method, or the logic of science, or to explore the interfaces of the fields of science, or to axiomatize the sciences—*e.g.* mathematics, physics —which are axiomatizable. In one sense the philosophy of science extends back to the origins of Western philosophy. From the origin of philosophy until the period of the

Sophists the emphasis of philosophy was on scientific knowledge. Plato and Aristotle devoted attention to science and its methods. But the development of Philosophy of Science as a discipline required a prior development of the sciences. Hence, it is more appropriate to regard philosophy of science as beginning with the remarkable development of the sciences in the modern period.

Phlogiston Theory. An 18th-century explanation of combustion which held that every combustible substance contained phlogiston. an inflammable material substance. Phlogiston was thought to be consumed in the process of combustion, leaving the original substance behind. Propounded by J.J. Becher and G.E. Stahl, the theory remained viable for a century until Lavoisier produced his counter theory involving oxygen Stahl, who defended the theory with great vigor, was influenced in the direction of animism and vitalism by J.B. Van Helmont.

Physicalism. Refers to the doctrine that all propositions asserting 'matters of fact and real existence' can be formulated as statements about publicty observable physical objects and activities (Hume's fork).

Physico-theological Argument. Kant's teleological argument for the existence of God.

Plato 428-348 B C Greek philosopher. Born in Athens. Studied under Socrates. Born of a distinguished Athenian family, he early intended to follow a political career, but the trial and death of Socrates turned him toward philosophy. After Socrate's death Plato left Athens, pending some time in travel, including a visit to his friend, Dion brother-in-law of the tyrant, Dionysius. According to the sources, he intended to use Syracuse as a pilot project for an experiment leading toward his perfect state. There is a legend that this visit ended in his being sole into slavery, and rescued by a friend. In any case, on his return to Athens in 388 he founded his famous Academy, the first true university offering a wide range of studies including all of the then extant sciences. In 367, upon the death of Dionysius I, Dion invited Plato back to supervise the education of Dionysius II Plato made a brief visit which succeeded at least in establishing a course of royal in struction in mathematics and philosophy. In 361 he visited Syracuse a third time, apparently hoping to gain approval for a federation of Greek city states against Carthage; but this trip, too, ended in failure. He returned to Athens, disappointed by his ventures in practical politics, continuing to spread the influence of the Academy until his death.

Principal writings: Apology; Crito; Euthyphro; Ion; Protagoras; Gorgias; Meno; Cratylus; Phaedo; Republic; Symposium; Parmenides; Sophist; Theaetetus; Phaedrus; Politicus; Philebus; Timaeus; Critias; and Laws.

Plato wrote dialogues for the public and lectures for his classes at the Academy. The works mentioned above are his dialogues; none of his lectures has survived (the exact opposite is true with respect to Aristotle). The dialogues are works of art, rich in figurative expression. Indeed, the mixture of metaphor and analysis has led some to find metaphor a working part of his method, both illustrating the analysis and serving as a place-marker for an analysis which for the present eludes the thinker. In both cases he regards metaphor and myth as particularly appropriate to the changing nature of the world of becoming, in contrast to the conceptual nature of the eternal world. There is a good deal of disagreement concerning (a) how we are to separate the work of Plato from that of Socrates, since Socrates appears as potagonist in most of Plato's dialogues; (b) whether Plato had a system of philosophy and if so what is its nature.

Platonism. As the philosophy deriving directly or indirectly from the work of Plato, Platonism can be seen as a commentary on complexities in Plato's own thought.

Plato's philosophy offers almost every obstacle to simple systematic exposition. He transmitted it to posterity principally through dialogues written over a period of 50 years, during which his thought developed considerably. Modern scholarship distinguishes between :

(1) the inclusive, aporetic dialogues of his early, so-called Socratic period,

(2) the great works of his middle period like the Phaedo and the Republic with their positive metaphysical, psychological, and political doctrines, and

(3) late writings like the Parmenides and the Sophist, in which these doctrines are subjected to radical reappraisal and modification. Even in his middle period, Plato's teachings tend to vary in detail and implications from one dialogue to another.

The central doctrine in this period, indeed the centre of Plato's whole work as a philosopher, is the theory of Forms or Ideas. These eternal transcendent realities directly apprehended by thought are contrasted with the transient contingent phenomena of our empirical existence. The Forms fulfil a number of barely compatible functions, appearing sometimes in the role of universals (universals and particulars), sometimes as ideal standards, sometimes as the intelligible model or blueprint of the sensible world. Plato's theory of substantive Ideas has to account singlehanded for a variety of facts—ontological, epistemological, and ethical. It shows a variety of philosophical influences, Heraclitean, Pythagorean, Parmenidean, and Socratic; it also reveals, like Plato's work as a whole, two contrasting motives; on the one hand, a poetic, religious awareness of an unseen eternal world, dimly reflected in the phenomena around us, and, on the other, a mathematical urge to analyse reality into its ultimate units. Doctrines of such complexity do not lend themselves readily to systematic exposition, which Plato anyway distrusted. The dialogue, with its dramatic elements, its ironies, its recourse to mythical figurative language, was his chosen literary vehicle for teachings that he was not propounding as a definitive system.

Plato's Academy C. 385 B.C. 529 A.D. The school founded by Plato in Athens. Named from the gardens in which the school was located, a public place dedicated to the Greek hero, Academus. The school specialized in the study of mathematics, music, astronomy, and dialectic. The history of the school may be divided into four parts, although some scholars prefer a tripartite division : the Ancient or First Academy; the Middle or Second Academy; the New or Third Academy; and the Very New or Fourth Academy. In the last stage, that of the Fourth Academy, the Academy is sometimes called the School of Athens and is part of the Neoplatonic movement.

Pleasure. Ultimately from the Greek hedone ('delight, enjoyment'). The doctrine that pleasure is the end of life, or that the pursuit of pleasure is built into man's nature, is called Hedonism. Pleasure has been often advanced as man's final value and pain his final disvalue, that we seek the one and shun the other. Aristotle regarded pleasure not as the end of activity, but as a concomitant of successful functioning.

Plenitude, Principle of. A phrase coined by A.O. Lovejoy to describe the notion that all possibilities are realized in the world. The entire created Universe is conceived of as a continuum in which there are no gaps, no dislocations ('Nature makes no leaps'), and no unrealized potentialities.

Plenum. Space totally filled with matter; the opposite of a vacuum. The concept featured in a number of cosmologies from the Stoics.

Pluralism. Any metaphysical view holding that the world must be composed of more than one or two basic kinds of entities. The latter views would be termed Monism or Dualism.

Plurality of Forms. Refers to a doctrine that held that bodies possessed a number of forms—of plants, of elements, etc., the form of light being the highest of these and responsible for generating all the rest.

Plurative Logic. The little known field of the logic of majorities, also called pleonoletic logic : if, for instance, 'Most as are Bs' and 'Most As are Cs', then necessarily 'Some B is C. It was Sir William Hamilton who first argued that 'most' is a quantifier on all fours with 'all', 'some', and 'no'.

Pneuma. A Greek term meaning 'air.' The term was used by Stoic philosophers as a principle of animation for the universe, and the term they preferred to psyche or soul, as the principle of animation in man as well.

Pneumatology (or Pneumatics). In the 17th and 18th centuries, a branch of metaphysics dealing with the theory and science of spiritual beings, which included God, the angels, and the human soul.

Poiesis. A Greek term signifying the activity of creating, making, or producing. In Aristotle poiesis defines one of the three types of science, the productive science; and poietic knowledge correspondingly is set in contrast to theoretical and practical knowledge.

Polar Concepts. Opposites such as immediacy and mediation, unity and plurality, ideal and real. The 'principle of polarity' advanced by M. R. Cohen states that members of such pairs are intelligible only in terms of contrast with each other.

Polarity, Principle of

(1) Nicholas of Cusa held that polar opposites apply at the same time to infinite beings. God is the chief example of the principle's applicability.

(2) Fichte. Hegel, and Marx and his followers, believed that such opposites were replaced by a synthesis in the process of dialectic.

Political Philosophy. Centering around the problem of the nature of society and of the state, considering not only how these entities are but how they ought to be ordered.

Plato envisioned a republic in which educational success determines one's role in society, even with respect to those who rule; and the just society has the same structure as the just soul, written large.

Where Plato made the developed individual the basic unit of society, Aristotle regarded the family as that unit. Nor is there a single preferred organization of the state. Instead, monarchy, aristocracy, and polity are the preferred forms of which tyranny, oligarchy, and democracy are the deformations.

Polity. In Aristotle one of the three desirable forms of government. Polity seemed to have been Aristotle's preference. It has many of the features of constitutional democracy.

Polysyllogism. A systematic series of syllogisms leading to a single conclusion.

Polytheism. From the Greek polys ('many') and theos ('god'). The view that there are many gods. Polytheism stands in contrast to henotheism and monotheism.

Pope. From the Greek papas ('father') Head of the Roman Catholic Church. Bearing the title Pontifex Maximus (meaning 'supreme intermediary between man and God'), the pope is regarded by Roman Catholics as successor to Peter as Bishop of Rome, and bearing in himself all of the powers Christ granted Peter. As of 1870 it was decided that infallibility characterized the pope's utterances when defining doctrines of faith and morals.

Port Royal. Cistercian abbey, home of the Jansenist community in 17th century France. The name was given to a system of logic developed by Arnauld, Nicole, and Pascal, which emphasized the need for careful definition of terms and concepts and laid the foundations of modern linguistic analysis. The first two produced the influential book L'Art de Penser (1662), usually known as the Port Royal Logic.

Positive Philosophy. A phrase introduced by Saint-Simon as a synonym for Positivism, a scientific approach to the world. Schelling meant by the term a positive approach to the universe, an approach which was mythological and spiritualistic in tone. With Comte the term. Positivism, became standard for the scientific approach.

Positivism. A family of philosophies characterized by an extremely positive evaluation of science and scientific method.

The term was introduced by Saint-Simon for whom the implications of the positive philosophy extended beyond philosophy to political, educational, and religious reforms. He found society alternating between critical and organic epochs.

Postulate. From the Latin term postulatum meaning 'demand,' request,' or 'claim.' The term is usually used to indicate those propositions which form the starting point of inquiry which are neither definitions, nor provisional assumptions, nor so certain that they can be taken as axiomatic. They are laid down as ture, and used without demonstration. Thus 'postulate' is one of a family of related terms including 'definition'. 'assumption' 'hypothesis' and 'axiom'.

Potentiality. From the Latin potentia, derived from potens, meaning 'to be powerful' in a certain respect or 'to have a capacity' of a certain kind. The Latin term is a translation of the Greek dynamis, used, by Aristotle as the name of the factor correlative to actuality in the analysis of change.

Pragmaticism. A term coined by C.S. Peirce in 1905 to denote his own particular variety of pragmatism, after the latter term had been appropriated and its scope widened by other philosophers.

Pragmatics. That branch of semiotics concerned with the relations between signs and their users, *i.e.*, with problems of signification.

Pragmatism. A label for a doctrine about meaning first made a philosophical term in 1878 by C.S. Peirce. 'Consider what effects, which might conceivably have practical bearings, we conceive the object of our conception to have. Then our conception of these effects is the whole of our conception of the object.' The term was soon borrowed by William James, F. C.S. Schiller, and John Dewey, who all in their different ways made pragmatism a theory of truth. Thus in his Pragmatism James said, 'Ideas become true just so far as they help us to get into satisfactory relations with other parts of our experience,' Peirce reacted by coining the substitute 'pragmaticism', a word too ugly to be purloined. Russell assailed the pragmatist notion of truth as obscurantist.

Prakriti. Sanskrit term which means 'matter' or 'substance.' Along with purusha, which stands for soul or spirituality, one of the two basic concepts of the Sankhya philosophy.

Pranayama. Sanskrit term meaning 'breath control.' The fourth step in Yogic meditation.

Pratyahara. Sanskrit term meaning 'sense-control.' The fifth step in Yogic meditation.

Preachers, Order of. Alternate name for the Dominican Order.

Precognition. In parapsychology, a word now having a particular reference to that kind of extrasensory perception (ESP) in which guesses, dreams, hunches, etc. precede their fulfilments. One philosophical problem is that the phenomena are seen as themselves being, or warranting, foreknowledge; which is taken either to make the future events inevitable or to show that they always must have been. The other philosophical issue is that precognitive ESP is often construed as involving backwards causation : perhaps because it is thought of on the model of perception, the 'fulfilment' is taken to be a causally necessary condition of the 'anticipation' (causal theory of perception).

Predestination. The doctrine that everything that happens, including particularly the making of all choices, has been fixed in advance by God : 'The first dawn of creation wrote what the last day of reckoning shall read.'

Predestination. The doctrine, that man's salvation or damnation was predetermined from eternity by God. When the doctrine holds that not only man's eventual disposition, but every event of his life is predestined, the position is identical to a special kind of determinism.

Predicable. From the Latin praedicare ('to proclaim or affirm'). The predicable is that which may be affirmed of something.

Predicaments. An obsolescent synonym for 'categories', in the Aristotelian sense.

Predicate In the traditional or subject-predicate logic, that which is affirmed or denied of a subject.

Predication. The act of affirming or denying a predicate of a subject. Where modern logic deals with classes, sets and relations, the logic of Aristotle is a logic of predication.

Predictability. The capability of being foretold. It means only and exactly what is says, and must therefore be distinguished from both predestination and causal determinism.

Prediction Paradox. Refers to the paradox of propositions that are falsified by the utterance of the prediction they announce.

Prejudice. Any belief, whether correct or incorrect, held without proper consideration of or sometimes in defianance of, the evidence.

Premise (or Premiss). In any argument, one of the statements from which another statement (the conclusion) is deduced or of which the conclusion is presented as a consequence.

Prescriptivism. The view that the primary function of moral judgement is to prescribe courses of action. R M. Hare, who coined the term. holds that if a statement is prescriptive then :

(a) Anyone who sincerely accepts it, and can act upon it does so act, and

(b) It cannot be entailed by a purely descriptive statement.

esent. The part of time lying between the past and the future

From Aristotle to Newton the present moment was an objective portion of the passage of time.

Pre-socratics. The name commonly given to the early period of Greek philosophy, covering the period from the middle of the 7th to the middle of the 5th century B.C.

Presupposing

(1) Collingwood regarded metaphysics are the study of the absolute presuppositions of a period of time.

(2) Strawson holds that certain difficulties in Russell's theory of definite descriptions can be avoided by keeping in mind that in referring to an entity, one presupposes, without asserting, existence.

Presupposition. An assumption that involves either a necessary or a contingent truth. If p is logically presupposed by q then it is a necessary truth that to deny the assumption p while asserting q would be a contradiction. Presuppositions that do not satisfy this requirement involve a contingent truth.

Pride. The Greek term is hybris. Along with concupiscence, pride is the source of sin in the Christian tradition. Often regarded as a mortal sin, pride implies a lack of dependence on God.

Prima Facie Obligations. The label popularized by Sir David Ross for those authentic moral claims that may on occasion be overridden by other and stronger moral claims.

Primary and Secondary Qualities. Primary qualities are those which things do actually have, secondary are only powers to produce experiences in us.

Private Language. A language for terms of which are defined to refer to the private sensations of the user, and whose meanings can therefore be known only to him.

Privation. The belief that evil is essentially negative—the lack of absence of good (privatio boni).

Privileged Access. The particular relationship we have to contents of our own consciousness, but that none of us has to the contents of anybody else's.

Probabilism. The doctrine that certainty is unattainable, held by the Skeptics including members of the Second Academy.

Probability. From the Latin probare ('to prove, to approve'). The Latin is a translation of the Greek **eulogon** ('reasonable or sensible'). The term thus refers to the likelihood of the happening of an event, or of the truth of a proposition. Where conclusions follow by necessity in deductive inference, they follow only by probability in induction. Probability theory has been developed into a very sophisticated discipline in modern mathematics.

Probability Theory. The mathematical theory of probability enables us to calculate the probability of some kind of event given the probability of others.

Problematic. A term in Aristotelian logic used to indicate the mode or modality of a proposition. A problematic proposition is one that asserts that something is possible, for example, 'It is possible that it will rain'.

Process Philosophy. A term sometimes applied to those philosophies stressing 'becoming' rather than 'being.'

Progress. In philosophy the conception of progress is to be contrasted with the view that the Golden Age was in the past, and with the view that time is eternal recurrence. Of course, in both West and East, views can be cited where the cycle of time includes periods of progress and of regress or decline.

Prolepsis. A Greek term which means 'anticipation' :

(1) In traditional logic the term referred to the anticipation of an objection, and one's response to it.

(2) Among the Stoics the term was used to refer to any one of the principles or 'common notions' which the soul contains, whether innately or from common experience.

Proof Theory. The syntactic study of formal systems that proceeds by examining the structure of the proofs that can be constructed within them.

Proper Names. Proper names may be confined to such terms as 'Socrates,' 'Plato,' 'Aristotle,' and 'Mr. Brown,' or extended to all terms which pick out a single individual. In either case, the function of proper names is to refer one to certain objects. They are, then, expected to have denotation.

Property. From the Latin proprius ('one's own,' 'proper'). The term has been used to mark out both what is common to all the members of a class, and that to which a person has a legal title.

Prophecy. From the Greek prophetein ('the gift of interpreting the will of the gods'). Interpreting the will of the god sometimes, but by no means always, implied the prediction of future events.

Proposition. From the Latin proponere ("to set forth or propose"). A proposition is, hence, an assertion which proposes or denies something, and is capable of being judged true or false.

Propositional Calculus. That part of logic concerned with the valid inferences and transformations which can be drawn from the relations of propositions to each other :

1. Philo of Megara was the first to work out the definition of material implication. In all other cases it is true. The definition is accepted today. It was worked out independently, however and only later discovered in Philo.
2. Chrysippus had worked out the definitions of Modus Ponens. These definitions likewise became part of the calculus; they had wide currency, and were developed by many different individuals

Propositional Function. A technical term due to Russell, used to denote that for which a predicate of predicate logic stands.

Proprium. (Latin for : a possession or characteristic). A characteristic peculiar to and dependent upon the essence of a species, but not a necessary part of its essence. Aristotle contrasted, in a way that is not entirely clear, proprium with accident.

Prosyllogism. A syllogism preliminary to another, its conclusion forming a premise of the syllogism which follows.

Protasis. A Greek term meaning "that which is put forward :

In Aristotle's logic, the premise of a syllogism, especially the major premise.

The conditional clause of an "if-then" statement. The second clause is the apodosis.

Protocol Sentence. A sentence consisting of an observation report describing directly given experience.

Protocol Statements. (German : Protokollsatze). According to the Vienna Circle, those, basic statements that are immediately verifiable by experience, mutually independent logically, and perhaps also incorrigible.

Prudence. From prudentia, the Latin translation of the Greek word, phronesis.

Socrates, viewed the term as the guarantee of virtue in the equation, "virtue is knowledge."

Psyche. A Greek term meaning "breath."

In Homer and in Greek life generally the psyche was a subtle, breath-like animating principle which left the body at death and continued to exist as a shade or shadow.

Psychokinesis or PK. Movement by the mind or soul, a term introduced in parapsychology to refer to the putative phenomenon in which a person moves some object without any physical contact with that object.

Psychologism. The theory that psychology is the foundation of philosophy, and that introspection is the primary method of philosophical enquiry.

Psychology. From the Greek psyche ('breath') and logos ('knowledge of'). The term psyche was used by Greek philosophers to refer to the vital principle in man.

Psychology, Philosophy of. Refers to the study of the philosophical implications of psychology and psychological research.

Psychophysical Parallelism. The view that mental (psychical) and bodily (physical) events occur in separate but parallel sequences.

Ptolemaic System. The theory which assumes that the earth is the fixed centre of the universe, surrounded by concentric spherical shells, seven of which are the paths of the moving heavenly bodies, the eighth and outermost accommodating the fixed stars.

Punishment. The word in its full and central sense may be defined as the intentional infliction by some authority upon an offender, of some penalty intended to be disagreeable, for some offence against rules authorized by that authority. The references to intention and to an authority are both essential.

Purusa (Sanskrit for : self, spirit). In general, the principle of consciousness in man or the Universe. But its exact function is variously conceived in the different systems of Indian philosophy.

Purva Mimamsa. Sanskrit term meaning 'the early revered thought'. The term refers to a school of Indian thought dealing with the earlier portions of the Vedas, as Uttara Mimamsa or Vedanta dealt with the later part :

(1) Liberation from rebirth leads in this system to life in heaven, and liberation is tied to the doing of one's duty.

(2) Since the source of information concerning duty is to be found in the Vedas, it is necessary that the Vedas be not simply the opinions of men. Accordingly, the Vedas are regarded as eternal. That is to say, there never was a time when they had not been written. The Vedas, hence, are without an author; and apparent references to authors are to be understood as references to individuals who explained certain portions of the Vedas, but did not compose them.

(3) The eternality of the Vedas seems to lead to a theory of language. If the Vedas are eternal, so must be the language of the Vedas. Hence, the relation between word and meaning is held to be non-conventional : there is a natural and inborn relation between the word and its denotation.

Pythagoreanism. Refers to the philosophical teachings and way of life associated with Pythagoras.

Q

Quadrivium. From the Latin quatuor ('four') and viae ('ways'). The four advanced studies—arithmetic, geometry, astronomy, and music—following the Trivium in the medieval curriculum.

Quaestio (Latin for : question). One of the two principal forms of philosophical writing in the Middle Ages, originating in the practice of oral debate in the universities.

Qualities, Primary and Secondary. The primary qualities of things are solidity, extension, figure, motion, rest, and number. The secondary qualities are colors, sounds, tastes, smells, etc.

(1) The distinction between the two types of qualities was first made by the Greek atomists Democritus 3; Epicurus 4).

(2) After a long period of neglect the distinction reappeared.

(3) The precise terminology, 'primary qualities', and 'secondary qualities', was introduced by the scientist Robert Boyle and picked up from Boyle by Locke.

(4) Berkeley called the distinction into question in such a way that from the standpoint of Berkeley's system all qualities became secondary. The consequence was loss of the concept of a material world, and the emergence of Berkeley's philosophy of immaterialism.

Quality

(1) One of Aristotle's basic categories, quality is 'that by virtue of which a thing is such and such.' A quality may be a habit, disposition, capacity, or the form and figure of a thing.

(2) In the traditional logic one speaks of the quality of categorical propositions. By this, one means their characteristic of being affirmative or negative (Proposition 1).

(3) Kant followed both Aristotle and the traditional logic by regarding quality as one of the basic categories while deriving from the characteristic mentioned in (2) above the sub-categories of Positive, Negative, and Limited.

(4) For Locke's treatment of the term Primary and Secondary Qualities.

Quantification Theory. In modern logic the method devised for expressing in symbolic form statements of a general nature.

Quantifier. The name given to operators '(x)' *i e.*, 'for all x', and '(Ex)' *i.e.* 'there is an x', in formal logic. By means of these operators and the Propositional Calculus more complex forms of reasoning, including all forms of the syllogism, can be expressed in logical notation.

Quantifier Shift Fallacy. The mistake of arguing from 'For all values of x there is some one (thing) y such that x bears F to y'—symbolically, (Ax) (Ey) (Fxy)—directly to the conclusion that 'There is one y such that for all values of x, x bears F to y—symbolically, (Ey) (Ax) (Fxy).

Quantity. From the Latin quantitas '(amount'), a translation of the Greek poson.

For Aristotle one of the basic categories. Quantity in his view is either discrete or continuous; if continuous, it is either a magnitude or a temporal span. Quantity is also further divisible into units of the same kind.

Quantum. From the Latin quantus ('how much'). Used in philosophy to refer to a finite and determinate quantity, the term has passed into physics where its reference is to the packets of energy, or quanta, of quantum mechanics.

Quantum Mechanics. A system of mechanics used to explain the behaviour of atoms, molecules, and elementary particles.

Quiddity. From the Latin quidditas referring to the 'whatness' of a thing The term was introduced in the Latin translations of Avicenna to express Aristotle's distinction of second substance, *i.e.*, what a thing is, in contrast to primary substance, *i.e.*, the individual thing itself Thus the usual sense of the term is as a synonym for form, nature, or essence.

Quinque Viaf. Latin phrase meaning 'five ways'.

Quintessence. In Aristotelian physics, the pure fifth element (Latin : quinta essentia), believed to be the component of heavenly bodies. It was distinguished throughout the medieval period from earth, air, fire, and water but was believed to be latent in them. Alchemists equating it with the prima material or first matter, from which the rest of the world was made, attempted to distil it from the other elements.

R

Rabbi. Hebrew term which means "my great one." The ordination title for authoritative teachers of Judaism.

Radhakrishnan, Sarvepalli. 1888-1975. Indian philosopher and statesman. Studied at Madras. Taught at Madras, Mysore, Calcutta, Benares, and Oxford. He has served as Ambassador, Vice-president, and President of the Republic of India. Seeking the unity of the world's religions and philosophies, his own Vedantic interpretation—taking Shankara as his point of departure—led to Idealism as his philosophic position.

Radical Philosophy. Refers to a movement started in the 1970s which is centring on a journal of the same name. The journal expresses concern that philosophy should be relevant, not trivial, and that more attention should be given to some continental movements and other relatively neglected areas. "The philosophers have only interpreted the world in various ways," Marx said in 1845, "the point, however, is to change it" (italics original). Compare Philosophical Radicals.

Rama Hindu deity. Along with Krishna one of the last two incarnations of Vishnu. Their followers constitute a considerable portion of the Hindu people and a majority of the Vishnuites. Rama is the hero of the great epic work, the Ramayana. In Books Two through Six, apparently the original portion of the work, Rama is described simply as the best of men, a dutiful son, loving husband, and possessor of every virtue. But he succeeds in apparently superhuman undertakings, and so came to be regarded as more than human. In Books One and Seven, regarded as later additions by the scholarly community, his divinity is acknowledged. Since Vishnu, too, had performed miraculous tasks on behalf of men *e g.*, destroying demons, there was reason for connecting Rama with Vishnu. The popularity of Rama as an incarnation of Vishnu has continued from the 10th century A D. to the present.

Ramanuja. 11th Cent. A D. Indian philosopher. Born in Bautapuri. Originally an adherent of the philosophy of Shankara, Ramanuja fell under the influence of Vaisnavism and finally became head of a school representing this opinion. Dedicating himself to working out the philosophical basis of the hymns of the Attars, Ramanuja became the philosopher for the bhakti, or devotional strand, of Hinduism. Taking Shankara as his opponent, much of his writing was polemical, directed toward refutation of Shankara's philosophy.

Principal writings : Commentaries on the Vedanta Sutras; Vedantatattvasara Vedarthasangraha.

Ramayana. One of the two great epics of Hinduism. Consisting of seven books and 50,000 lines, the Ramayana is both older and shorter than its companion, the Mahabharata. Written between the 6th and 4th centuries B.C., the poem tells the story of the birth, youth, marriage, and exile of Prince Rama; the abduction of his wife by a demon and her return; his reign, final years, and death. As a morality tale, the story depicts the victory of Rama over his enemies, both natural and supernatural, through exemplary behavior. Interpolations in the 2nd century B C. transformed the story into one concerning Rama, the incarnation of Vishnu. On this level the poem becomes devotional literature, telling of the love and protection which Rama-Vishnu provides for those who trust Him.

Ramsey Sentence. The sentence generated, after the sentences of a scientific theory have been conjoined together, by replacing the theoretical term with variables and existentially quantifying into the result In plain terms the sentence reproduces the structure of the theory, and its empirical consequences, but removes the impression that we are dealing with understood theoretical items and properties.

Randomness. The situation that arises when, in repetitions of a trial in which there is a known, fixed probability of a particular result, there is no rule for predicting that result that tends towards any different success rate.

Rational

1. Opposed to irrational.
2. Opposed to non-rational or arational. Those who have spoken of man as the rational animal have of course been employing the word in the second sense, meaning capable of either rationality or irrationality, not trying to make it true by definition that everyone in fact achieves the one rather than the other.

Rationalism. From the Latin ratio ("reason"). The principle that reason is to be granted the primary role in explanation.

Realism

1. (in scholastic philosophy). The view that universals (universals and particulars) have a real substantial existence, independently of being thought. Duns Scotus was the most able supporter of this position.
2. (in modern philosophy) Most commonly the view that physical objects exist independently of being perceived. Thus understood, realism obviously reaffirms the standpoint of common sense, and it achieves the status of a philosophy only because a case against it has been seriously argued.

Reality. From the Latin realitas, deriving from res ("thing").

The Indian philosopher, Nagarjuna, looked upon reality as beyond intellect, the non-dual Absolute in which all distinctions merge.

Reason. From the Latin ratio ("reckoning").

Applied to a capacity in man to draw logical conclusions, a long tradition has regarded reason as man's most distinctive faculty.

Rebellion. Man's individual opposition to the state, as contrasted with revolution.

Rebirth. The general term, referring to a succession of births, of which Reincarnation is one basic modification. Reincarnation implies the notion of rebirth while denying the existence of soul.

Recursive. A term in formal logic and mathematcis, applied to definitions and functions. A recursive definition of a function or predicate defines it (1) explicitly as applied to the first term in a series and (2) for any successor term, via the predecessors of that term.

Recursive Function. Any function containing a hereditary property such that when the value of the function has been determined for one member of a series it is determinable for the next member of the series.

Redemption. From the Latin redemptio, from redimere ("to buy"). The doctrine that man is ransomed from sin by the divine. It has its most specific form in Christianity.

Reductio Ad Absurdum. The Latin phrase, meaning "reduction to absurdity." applies to a method of indirect proof in which one deduces a contradiction from the contradictory of the proposition to be proven.

Reductio Ad Impossibile. Latin phrase meaning "reduction to the impossible." A form of argument which seeks to establish the truth of a proposition by showing that the contradictory of that proposition involves impossible consequences; a form of the reductio ad absurdum.

Reductionism (or Reductivism)

1. Refers to the belief that human behaviour can be reduced to or interpreted in terms of that of lower animals; and that, ultimately, can itself be reduced to the physical laws controlling the behaviour of inanimate matter.

2. More generally, any doctrine that claims to reduce the apparently more sophisticated and comple to the less so.

Reduction Sentence. A device introduced by Carnap in order to solve the problem of scientific terms that resist explicit definition, such as those denoting dispositional properties.

Reference, Theory of. An area of contemporary philosophic concern over problems of denotation, or how words and phrases refer.

Referent In logic the first term of a relation whose second term is called the "relatum." If A has the relation R to B, A is the referent and B the relatum.

Reflexivity. The property of those relations in terms of which an entity relates to itself.

Reformation. The term is used to describe movements seeking to correct abuses in an established order, often by reverting to the principles and customs of an earlier period.

Refute. Strictly, not only to deny but also to provide sufficient reason for believing that what is denied is in fact false.

Regeneration. From the Latin regeneratus ('to have been born again'). In religion a new, spiritual birth.

Reification The fallacy of regarding a mental entity as though it were a thing.

Reincarnation. The doctrine that the soul becomes incarnate in a succession of bodies until by the necessary purification, or the using up of one's karma final release from the body occurs. A characteristic of Hinduism.

Reism. The attempt to preserve an objectivity for all kinds of intentional entities, exemplified in the philosophies of Brentano and Meinong.

Relation. The connection that a thing has, or the reference an idea makes, to other things or ideas.

Relations, Internal and External. If an individual X has a property which is such that, by virtue of having that property, X necessarily has a relation R to a certain thing or things, then R is an internal relation of X. But if X has a relation R to a certain thing or things, and there is no property of X such that, by virtue of having that property, X necessarily has this relation, then R is an external relation of X.

Relations, The Logic of. The logic of relations is that part of logic concerned with the expression of relational ideas, where *e.g*, some 'x' has the relation R to 'y'. This may be expressed either as 'xRy' or 'R(x, y)'.

Relativism. The doctrine that no absolutes exist.

In its epistemological application, the doctrine holds that all truth is relative.

Ethical relativism holds that there are no absolute criteria for formal judgments.

Relativity. A scientific principle, established in two parts by Albert Einstein. The first part (1905), special relativity, refers to non-accelerated systems and has immense philosophical implications both in respect to the extent to which it upsets the classical notions of time and motion and more specifically because of its impact on the concept of simultaneity.

The second part of Einstein's theory (1915), general relativity, deals with relative motion between accelerated systems. It makes further extensive modifications to our concepts of space and time, treating them as a non-Euclidean continuum, 'curved' by the presence of matter in such a way that gravitation appears as a consequence of the geometry of the Universe.

Space and time are concepts that form part of the models we construct to represent the real world. But not all concepts have a counterpart in reality : atoms probably do, phlogiston certainly does not. Relativity has made us modify our concepts of space and time and with it our model of reality : it has also made us reconsider some of the underlying concepts of epistemology itself.

Religion. From the Latin religare ('to bind fast'), typically the term refers to an institution with a recognized body of communicants who gather together regularly for worship, and accept a set of doctrines offering some means of relating the individual to what is taken to be the ultimate nature of reality.

Religion, Philosophy of. The philosophy of religion is not primarily concerned either to promote or to discourage such belief, or to add to our factual knowledge of religious history or psychology or the detailed differences between sects and traditions. Rather it is concerned to analyse the special roles played, and the special problems raised, by the characteristic concepts and doctrines of religion within the whole structure and economy of human thought.

Reminiscence (or Recollection), Argument from. Plato's argument that certain kinds of knowledge could not have been acquired in this life, but involve the recollection (Greek : anamnesis) of a previous acquaintanceship with the Forms or Ideas.

Reminiscence, Doctrine of. From the Greek term anamnesis. Plato's doctrine of knowledge as recollection.

Renaissance Originally a French word meaning 'rebirth' or 'revival.' Applied to the period of time in Western Europe running from the 14th through the 16th centuries, the term became current after Michelet in 1855 and Burckhardt in 1860 used the term in titles of historical works on France and Italy, respectively.

Representamen. That which represents, or stands for, another.

Representation. The act or relation of representing.

Representationalism (or Representationism). A generic term that broadly refers to theories of perception wherein the sensing mind is believed not to have direct acquaintance with its objects, but to apprehend them through the medium of ideas that are supposed to represent those objects.

Representative Theory of Ideas. The view that the mind knows reality only through the mediation of ideas.

Representative Theory of Perception. The view that is also known as representationalism or representationism.

Resemblance. One of the basic principles of association. By virtue of resemblance one mental object calls up another. Russell held 'resemblance' to be the one universal indispensable to the life of the mind.

Resistentialism A fictitious school of fashionable continental philosophy invented by Paul Jennings in 1948. This particular and popular invention is often wrongly included among the many similar contributions of Michael Frayn, consequent upon his undergraduate work in philosophy at Cambridge.

Responsibility. The notion that a person is answerable for his actions and so is a proper subject for praise or blame.

Responsibility Moral. The view that one is answerable for his actions in terms of a moral or ethical criterion. The traditional view is that responsibility implies that man has free will.

Resurrection. The doctrine that the dead shall rise in bodily form. To be distinguished from the idea of Immortality which supposes an eventual separation of soul from body.

Retrodiction. The inverse of prediction, referring to the process by which one makes an inference into the past on the basis of present knowledge.

Revelation. The term usually refers to an unveiling of truths which could not be reached by reason alone. The term stands in contrast to reason much as does its correlative term, 'faith'.

Rhetoric. From the Greek rhetor ('orator'). A discipline, historically related to philosophy, dealing with the principles of persuasion.

Richard's Paradox. A paradox presented by Jules Richard in 1905. It involves a diagonal argument concerning denoting phrases and what they denote and thus considered to be one of the semantic paradoxes.

Right. The 'right' and the 'good' are key terms in the study of Ethics. The former is sometimes defined as 'what ought to exist in its own right,' and the latter as 'what one ought to do.' An ethical theory can be said to be shaped to some extent by the decision as to which concept is dominant in the theory.

Rights. A person's entitlements as a member of society, including 'liberties', such as the right to use the public highway and 'claim rights', such as the right to defence counsel.

Rigid Designator. An expression that designates the same thing in every possible world.

Rig veda. The most important of that division of the Vedas called the Samhitas. The Samhitas are collections of scripture containing hymns and prayers to the Vedic Gods. The Rig veda, one of four such collections, consists of ten books and was completed before 800 B C.

Rin. Japanese, term meaning 'companionship.

Romanticism A reaction against the rationalism and empiricism of the period of the Enlightenment, romanticism is best characterized by its idealist celebration of the self, by its respect for the transcendental, and by its conviction of the power of the imagination and of the supreme value of art.

Rosicrucianism. A movement for political reform and spiritual regeneration that originated in early 17th century Germany. It centred on a fictitious religious society reputedly founded by a certain Christian Rosenkreuz in 1484. The philosophical content of its teachings is heavily coloured by alchemy, mysticism, and occultism.

Rudra. The maleficent storm god of the Vedic religion. Rudra brings the destructive aspects of the storm. He likewise inflicts diseases, but also heals them.

Rule of Inference. The formula or argument form whereby the conclusion follows from a premise or set of premises.

Russell. Bertrand Arthur William (1872—1970). British philosopher. He subsequently held a variety of university posts in Cambridge and elsewhere, interspersed with other pursuits, literary, educational, and political. From his long list of publications the following may be picked out as philosophically the most important : The Philosophy of Leibniz (1900). The Principles of Mathematics (1903), Principia Mathematica (with A.N. Whitehead, 3 volumes, 1910-13). The Problems of Philosophy (1912), Our knowledge of the External World (1914), The Analysis of Mind (1921), The Analysis of Matter (1927), An Enquiry into Meaning and Truth (19 0). Human Knowledge : Its Scope and Limits (1948), and Logic and Knowledge (a collection of some of his most important essays) (1956).

Russell's Paradox. An important paradox in set theory. Some sets (classes or collection) are members of themselves and some are not. For instance, the set of horses is not a number of itself since it is a set and not a horse, whereas the set of non-horses is a member of itself.

S

Sabellianism. The doctrine of Sebellius that Father, Son, and Holy Spirit are the same Being. The name refers loosely to all interpretations of the Godhead which are more unitarian than trinitarian.

Sacerdotalism. From the Latin sacerdos ('a priest'). Any religious system revolving around the priestly order, or the doctrine that ordination confers special powers and rights.

Sadducism (or Sadduceeism). The beliefs of the Jewish sect to Sadducees, active around the time of Christ, particularly in so far as they concerned denial of the resurrection of the body and the existence of spirits.

Sagehood. The goal of life in neo-Confucian philosophy. Mencius held that everyone has the capacity to become a Sage.

Salvation. From the Latin salvare ('to save'). The Christian term for that state in which man is redeemed, and reconciled to God. The mediator in this event is Jesus Christ, who atones for man's sins.

Salva Veritate. (Latin for : the truth being preserved.) A condition of synonymy, first formulated by Leibniz. Expressions are synonymous (or may be said to have the same meaning) if they are mutually substitutable without altering the truth-value of the statement in which they occur.

Samadhi. Sanskrit term meaning 'concentration'. The eighth and final step in the path of Yogic meditation leading to liberation.

Samkhya. The most archaic of the systems of Indian philosophy.

Samsara (Sanskrit for: transmigration.) The doctrine, characteristic of all Indian religions, of an almost endless cycle of death and rebirth.

Sankhya. One of the six orthodox systems of Indian philosophy, arising in response to the Vedas and the heterodox systems. The system is attributed to Kapila, who is said to have lived in the 7th century B.C.

Sannyasi. A Sanskrit term meaning 'one who renounces.' The term refers to the fourth or mendicant stage of the Brahman religious life.

Sarvastivada. One of the three main schools of Hinayana Buddhism.

Sat, Chit, Ananda. Sanskrit phrase meaning 'Being, Intelligence, and Bliss.' Although Brahman is at times said to be without characteristics, or beyond characterization, these three terms are often taken to characterize the divine consciousness in Hindu philosophy.

Satisfaction. A technical term in formal semantics; the condition in which an object, or sequence of objects, 'satisfies' a predicate, that is, the predicate is true of that object, or sequence of objects.

Scepticism. In a general sense and with a small s, the philosophical attitude that maintains that sure knowledge of how things really are may be sought, but cannot be found. Scepticism (with a capital S) is the name attached to a particular school of ancient Greek philosophy.

Schema. Greek term meaning 'diagram'.

In Kant's philosophy (Kant 11c), the term refers to the exercise of the 'Transcendental Imagination', bringing sense and understanding together in particular ways to produce various essential concepts.

Scholasticism. The kind of philosophy practised in the schools of the medieval universities. The roots of the term stretch back to the Greek word for 'leisure', since it was recognized from antiquity that for the contemplation of the ultimate reasons for things, leisure is an essential condition. The adjective 'scholastic' is also applied to medieval theology.

School of Athens. c. 380 (?)-529. The name given to Plato's Academy after its conversion to Neoplatonism.

Science, Philosophy of Organized empirical science provides the most impressive result of human rationality and is one of the best accredited candidates for knowledge. The philosophy of science seeks to show wherein this rationality lies; what is distinctive about its explanations and theoretical constructions; what makes it off from guesswork and pseudo-science and makes its predications and technologies worthy of confidence; above all whether its theories can be taken to reveal the truth about a hidden objective reality.

Scientism

(1) The belief that the human sciences require no methods other than those of the natural.

(2) In a more general sense, practices that pretend to be, but are not, science.

Scope. Of a logical operator, the shortest propositional function in which it occurs.

Seafight. The problem set by Aristotle in De Interpretatione IX. Since it is clearly necessary that either there will be a seafight tomorrow or there will not, surely whichever in fact happens must happen necessarily and inevitably.

Secondary Causes. Ordinary, everyday causes 'within the Universe' seen in relation to and in contrast with the First Cause.

Secularism. From the Latin saecularis ('the times', 'the age', 'the world'). The secular stands in contrast to the sacred, marking an approach to life divorced from the influence of religion, and thus determined by temporal or wordly concerns.

Secundum Quid. Latin phrase meaning 'according to something'. It is used in Scholastic terminology as a qualifying phrase. An assertion secundum quid is to be taken in a qualified, restricted, or secondary sense. Failure to take an assertion in its properly restricted sense is sometimes called the fallacy of secundum quid.

Seelenfunklein. Eckhart (3).

Sefiroth Cabala (Ib).

Seienden. Heidegger (5).

Self. An obsolescent technical term for a person, but a person thought of as incorporeal and essentially conscious.

Self-contradiction. The affirmation by the same person of two propositions that are in contradiction, or contradictory, one to the other. What that person has thus said is self-contradictory.

Self-deception. A state resembling but distinguishable from that of ignorance or of false belief, and consisting in a motivated blindness to facts that are in some way or for some reason undesirable or unacceptable to the individual concerned.

Self-determination. The determination of one's actions by onself without external compulsion.

Self-regarding. A term applied by J.S. Mill to actions that affect only the agent, to be contrasted with not self-regarding (or other-regarding) actions.

Self-realization. The development of the possibilities of the self.

Semantic Paradoxes. Usually distinguished from the logical paradoxes in that they arise from the use of semantic notions such as truth and reference.

Semantics (in general). The study of signs and their relations to what they signify. 'Semiosis' and 'semiotics' are also used in this sense.

Semiotics The theory of signs; also called semiology'. It is traditionally divided into three parts : syntactics, the study of grammar; semantics, the study of meaning, and pragmatics, the study of the actual purposes and effects of meaningful utterances.

Sensa. A wide term covering all the locutions used in the perennial attempts to differentiate, from what publicty exists and is actually perceived, that which is merely felt, and the feeling of which does not, of itself, imply that anything either exists or has any specifiable qualities.

Sensation

1. Ordinarily, having such feelings as cold, pressure, thirst, itches, or pains.

2. Technically, mental entities of a kind private to their owner.

Sensationalism. A term sometimes used in the history of philosophy to designate those who hold that all knowledge has its origin in sensation.

Sense Data. See sense datum.

Sense-datum. A term referring to that which is immediately given in awareness. The plural is sense-data.

Sense Experience The portion of a living agent's history that is derived from reception of stimuli through the five senses; or, a or single identifiable and unified body of such stimuli.

Sensibilia (sing sensibile). A term for sense data thought to exist unsensed.

Sensible World. The world as we have access to it in sense experience.

Sensor

1. An organ of sense in a living thing, that receives stimuli.

2 A whole organism that is, among other things, capable of receiving stimuli.

Sensorium. Both the Greek and Latin terms were used to refer to whatever was regarded as the organ in man where sensations came together in forming the representation of an object.

Sensum. Plural 'sensa'. Terms referring to the immediately given in awareness.

Separation of Powers. The separation of powers into legislative, executive, and judicial, made concrete in the American Constitution, was recommended by Montaigne.

Set. A set is a collection of objects known as the members or elements of the set.

Set Theory. The theory of sets was initiated by Cantor and stands at the interface of logic and mathematics. The discipline has moved through many controversies whose locus has centered in the logical paradoxes concerning sets which are and at the same time are not members of themselves. One solution is that of axiomatic set theory.

Shinto Japanese transliteration of two ideograms meaning 'the way of the gods'. The term refers to the set of religious practices, relating to local shrines, and directed to indigenous Japanese deities.

Shiva. Hindu god. Center of worship in the Saiva sect of Hinduism. In the Hindu trinity he is the destroyer, while Brahma creates, and Vishnu preserves. His wife is Kali, a destroyer goddess, who is worshipped as the terrible mother. Shiva's symbol is the linga or phallus; the bull is associated with his worship. He is also the god of mountains and of the overcoming of death. The contrasting ascriptions given to Shiva as destroyer and redeemer may relate to differences of tradition, the former originating in the north and the latter in the south of India.

Shunyavada. Sanskrit term meaning 'criticism'. The core term, shunya, literally means 'negation' or 'void', but is better taken as 'indescribable'. Shunyavada is the name of one of the most important of the schools of Buddhism.

Sign. From the Latin signum and the Greek semeion, originally meaning a verbal signal. The theory of signs is usually called Semiotic.

Simple Enumeration. An inductive method. If this A and that A and the other A are all θ, and these are all the As which you are acquainted with, then it is an induction by simple enumeration to conclude that all As are θ.

Signification. Most often used as synonymous with 'meaning', 'connotation', or 'intension'.

Simplicity. The contemporary equivalent of Ockham's Razor is the view held by philosophers of science that simplicity is one of the criteria determining the selection of the primitives or undefined predicates at the base of a conceptual system.

Sin. Strictly, a theological term, meaning offence against God. What is a sin, therefore, may or may not violate thisew-worldly moral standards.

Social Contract. Refers to an agreement between individuals, or between individuals and a governing power, in which some personal liberties are freely surrendered in return for the advantages of having a well-organized society, or good government.

Social Contract Theory. The doctrine that social organization rests on a contract or compact which the people have made among themselves.

Social Darwinism. The belief that the development and structure of human societies can be explained in terms of the evolutionary forces that shape non-human biology, and particularly in terms of "survival of the fittest".

Socialism. From the Latin 'socius ('comrade'). The term applies to any association, private or public, organized around the principle of group control of property and the production and distribution of wealth.

Social Philosophy. An expression afflicted with the same vagueness and ambiguity as besets the word 'philosophy' itself, as well as with other troubles of its own.

Society. Translation of the Latin societas from socio ('to share or to unite').

Aristotle does make a distinction between state and society since his state is composed of societal units, that is, of families.

Sociology. From the Latin socio ('to associate') and logos (knowledge)'. The term is taken to refer to a study of the forms, institutions, functions, and interrelations of human groups.

Sociology of Knowledge. A misnamed discipline, which is in fact devoted to discovering the social causes of people having whatever beliefs they do have, without prejudice to the quite different question of whether they have, or there are, sufficient grounds to warrant rating these beliefs as knowledge.

Socratic Fallacy. The mistake, characteristic of the Socrates of Plato's earlier dialogues, of arguing that no one knows anything about Xs. or even that any Xs truly are Xs, unless he can provide a definition of the word 'X'.

Socratic Method. The dialectical method supposedly employed by the historical Socrates, and displayed in Plato's earlier dialogues.

Socratic Schools. The term is used to refer to schools of philosophy shaped by the influence of Socrates. In this sense Plato's Academy would qualify as one of the Socratic schools; but the mature Platonic thought is, rather, considered as initiating its own school.

Salipsism. From the Latin solus ("alone") and ipse ("self"). The doctrine that the individual human mind has no grounds for believing in anything but itself.

Soma. A god of the Vedic religion. Initially an intoxicating beverage of ancient India, Soma by personification became a god.

Some. Traditionally in logic, at least one and perhaps as many as all but one.

Sophists From the Greek sophistes ('one who professes to make men wise'). Today the term is applied almost exclusively to a remarkable group of teachers in 5th-century B.C. Athens. Markedly different in method, interests, and goals from the cosmological speculations of Greek philosophy's initial period, the Sophists centered their interest in language, rhetoric, education, and questions of social philosophy.

Sorites. An argument with any number of premises and terms that otherwise satisfy the criteria for syllogisms, and can be set out as a series of syllogisms each of whose conclusions forms one premise of the succeeding syllogism.

Soul. In one sense, the principle of life, defined as what makes living things alive. The Greek word for 'alive', like the equivalent Latin word 'animatus' and its English derivative 'animate', is etymologically the same as 'ensouled'; this is the ancient connection between the ideas of soul and of life. Plato, presumably following Socrates, both identified the soul with the person who reasons decides, and acts, and assumed that this person or soul is not the familiar creature of flesh and blood but rather the incorporeal occupant and director of, even the prisoner in, that corporeal being.

Sovereignty. From the French souverain referring to the 'chief' or 'supreme' power of the state.

Space. Along with time, one of the ultimate categories of natural philosophy.

Greek philosophy contrasted the plenum and the void. Where Democritus used the void as his concept of space, that in which atoms move, Parmenides held there could be no empty space, since, as his disciple Zeno of Elea argued, the concept is contradictory; he therefore interpreted space as a plenum; its fullness, indeed, makes motion impossible.

Einstein developed the concept of the relativity of space, and discovered its curvature. The relativity of space-time means that simultaneity can be established only within a given intertial system, and has no validity for observers in systems moving in relation to the given inertial system.

Space-Time. A four-dimensional order with four coordinates, three of them spatial and one temporal. Specification of the co-ordi nates precisely locates any physical magnitude whatever

Species. A Latin term meaning 'sort' or 'kind.' The Greek is eidos ('form' or 'figure'); the term designates a class standing between the genus and the individuals to which the term refers.

Specious Present. The least temporal interval such that two modifications of experience, separated by that interval, may nevertheless seem to the subject to be co-present in his consciousness.

Speech Acts. Acts performed when words are uttered. J. L. Austin claimed that the complex act of uttering words involves various simple component acts.

Spirit. A word commonly used to translate the Hegelian term Geist (also translated as 'mind'). According to Hegel, spirit differs from nature in that spirit is an 'I'; in Hegel's language, spirit has being 'for itself'. Hegel recognizes three type of spirit : subjective, objective, and absolute.

Spiritualism. A term with both philosophical and religious associations. Philosophically, the term is sometimes used as a synonym of Idealism. In religion the term sometimes refers to the indwelling of the Holy Spirit.

Spontaneity. From the Latin sponte meaning 'of free will" or 'voluntarily.'

Square of Opposition. In medieval texts, a diagram summarizing the logical relations between the four categorical propositions each having the same subject and predicate terms These propositions are traditionally represented by A.E I.O.

State. From the Latin status ('standing' or 'position'). A collective entity with territorial boundaries and political organization exercising sovereign power.

State Description. In extensional semantics a class comprising, for a given semantical system, every atomic sentence or its negation. A true state description contains all of the true atomic sentences of the system, and the negation of all of the false atomic sentences.

State of Nature. Refers to the condition in which people either did live before, or would live without, making or acceding to a social contract.

Statistics. The science of handling information about classes of things, or populations, where each member is associated with one of a set of possible properties or outcomes.

Stimulus Meaning. A concept used by Quine in an attempt to explicate analyticity and synonymy in terms of behavioral dispositions. In addition to the above term he referred to stimulus-analyticity and stimulus-synonymy.

Stochastic. Denoting a physical process that gives rise to a class of events within which a characteristic has a definite probability; that is, a random variable takes on a defined distribution.

Stochastic Process. A process whose development is probabilistic, that is whose stages are determined by the values of one or more random variables.

Stoicism. From the Greek stoa ('porch'). A Graeco-Roman School of philosophy founded in 108 B.C. in Athens by Zeno of Citium, and developing its greatest influence in the Roman Empire where at one time it was the dominant intellectual influence. The name of the school derives from the location in Athens where the school first met. The doctrines of the school are diverse but they includ e the development of a logic (divided into rhetoric and dialectic), physics, and an ethic which likewise involves a theology. Indeed, the Stoics seem to have introduced the division of philosophy into these three disciplines.

Stratonician Presumption. The claim that it is up to anyone wanting to postulate a God (or any other initiating or sustaning principle outside and beyond the Universe) to show sufficient reason for so doing. Why cannot the Universe's existence and fundamental characteristics be themselves the ultimates of explanation ? The Five Ways of St. Thomas Aquinas are deployed to meet and, hopefully, to defeat two objections, one of which is in effect a statement of this presumption. The name refers to Strato of Lampsacus.

Straw Man. A position, not in fact held by an opponent in an argument, which is invented and assailed in preference to attending to his actual stance.

Stream of Consciousness. A phrase coined by the psychologist William James as a characterization of the mind, that is, that it is a process of continuous though.

Strict Implication. Implication and entailment.

Structuralism. A method of approach, rather than a distinct philosophy, that has application in both linguistics and the social sciences :

1. (In linguistics). The theory that language is best described, in terms of its irreducible structural units in morphology phonology, etc. Structure, deep and surface.

2. (In the social sciences). The view that the key to the understanding of observed phenomena lies in the underlying structures and systems of social organization.

Structuralism. An interdisciplinary point of view, philosophy, or philosophic movement of the present day whose central tenet is that all societies and cultures possess a common and invariant structure.

Structure, Deep and Surface. Terms occurring in Chomsky's analysis of grammar. This analysis supposes that speakers possess rules for combining various grammatical elements, such as verbs, tense signs, and nouns, into sequences. These initially unidiomatic strings (the deep, underlying structure) are then converted into vernacular speech by transformation rules. They thus take on the surface structurers of everyday speech.

Sturm UND Drang. A German phrase meaning storm and stress." A movement in Germany opposing the principles of Romanticism to the French ideals of Enlightenment.

Subaltern. A statement q is a subaltern of the statement p iff q is true whenever p is true and p is false whenever q is false.

Subconscious. A mental state or process occurring just below the level of awareness.

Subcontraries. A pair of statements that can be simultaneously true but which cannot be simultaneously false.

Subjectivism and Objectivism. Subjectivism. In its simplest form, the position held by someone who believes that all moral attitudes are merely a matter of personal taste.

Objectivism. The belief that there are certain moral truths that would remain true whatever anyone of everyone thought or desired.

Subject-Predicate Logic. Aristotle's logic of predication centering in the theory of the syllogism.

Sublime, the

(1) That which is beyond all comparison great, either mathematically in terms of limitless magnitude, or dynamically in terms of limitless power.

(2) The term used to designate natural objects that inspire a kind of awed terror through sheer immensity.

Subsistence. Subsistence is thought of as a monochrome and insubstantial analogue possessed by universals, numbers, and the difference between red and green.

Substance. The term refers to the underlying, supporting substratum of change. But 'substance' also contains the idea of the individual subject to change.

Substrate (or Substratum). Refers to that which bears properties. For example, the subject of any change between a pair of opposites, such as the material without which heat cannot itself change into cold, is a substrate.

Sudras. The laboring class of Indian tradition.

Sufficient Reason, Principle of. In Leibniz the view that nothing takes place without a reason sufficient to determine why it is as it is and not otherwise.

Suicide. The act of voluntarily taking one's own life. The case enters into discussions of freedom and responsibility.

Sui Generis. (Latin for : of its (or his or her) own kind.) Of a thing believed to be unique. and not a members of a class with other fellow members. God is often said to be sui generis.

Summum Bonum. A Latin term meaning 'the highest good'. The term has been applied to the ultimate ends of man, or to that which is intrinsically good.

Supernaturalism. The theological doctrine that the divine is fundamentally different from the temporal order and cannot be approached through its categories, *i.e*, by means of reason.

Supervenient Characteristics. Properties or qualities that depend on some other property or quality.

Suppositio. Latin term referring to the specific signification of a sign.

Surplus Value. According to Marx the difference between the price paid for a product and the price paid labor in its manufacture.

Syllogism. As defined by Aristotle, the founder of the traditional formal logic, a discourse in which, certain things being stated, something other than what is stated follows of necessity from their being so'.

Symbol In religious thought and practice, symbols are commonly regarded as sensuous representations of a transcendent reality. In systems of logical and scientific thought the term is normally used in the sense of an abstract sign.

Symmetry. A property of certain relations and matching geometrical elements. A relation is symmetrical when it is reversible.

Syncategorematic. In traditional logic, denoting a word that cannot stand on its own, but must be joined to a categorematic term in order to enter a categorical proposition, for example, 'all', 'and', and 'some'. In modern logic the sense has been extended to apply to any symbol that has no independent meaning.

Synderesis (or synteresis). In Aquinas and other scholastic writers, the innate intellectual quality that enables every man to intuit the general and basic principles of practical moral reasoning.

Syndicalism. A trade union movement, originating in France, according to which the 'syndicates' were to gain control over the means of production by the general strike and direct action.

Synonym. One of two or more words with the same meaning; for example 'donation' is synonymous with 'gift'.

Synonymy. The study of identity of meaning, especially as it touches upon the interpretation of analytic statements and the interchangeability of terms.

Syntactics. One of the three major aspects of the general theory of signs, along with Semantics and Pragmatics. Syntactics deals with that aspect of the study concerning the relations of the signs of a language to each other.

Syntax (of a natural language). The system of rules governing the grammatical construction of sentences of the language.

Synthesis. The term once designated deductive reasoning, but now stands as the complement of analysis, referring to the joining of separate elements into a whole.

Synthetic A Priori Judgment, Statement, or Proposition. A judgment, statement, or proposition in which the predicate adds content to the subject, and which yet has the necessity of analytic judgments.

System

(1) The term is sometimes applied to the characteristic features of the thought of particular individuals and schools, *e.g.*, Plato's system.

(2) In formal terms, by system is meant a set of elements with internal coherence and unity, provided by rules governing their permissible combination and transformation.

System of Logic. Any set of axioms and/or rules of inference governing some or all of the logical operators. The formal validity of an argument containing those logical operators can be checked by reference to such a system.

T

Tables of Induction. The tables of Essence and Presence, Absence in Proximity, and Degrees or Comparison, recommended by Francis Bacon in using inductive method.

Tabu. A polynesian term signifying a mysterious potency thought to involve danger to oneself or one's group.

Tabula Rasa. A phrase used by Locke to describe the state of the human mind at birth. His contention was that innate a priori knowledge is a fiction and that only experience can furnish the mind with ideas.

Tabula Rasa. A Latin term meaning 'blank tablet', the concept that the mind begins without innate knowledge, gaining all knowledge from experience.

Tagore, Rabindranath 1861-1941. Indian poet and philosopher. Born in Calcutta. Educated in London. Founded Visabharati

University. His many volumes of poetry were influenced by Bhakti-oriented Bauls of Bengal. His philosophical work was directed toward those central truths which mediate among all positions, or the 'one great principle of unity' in everyone. The following books were written in English.

Selected writings : Sadhana. The Realisation of Life, 1913; Personality, 1917; Creative Unity, 1922; The Religion of Man, 1931; Man, 1937; Towards Universal Man, 1961.

T'AI Chi. Chinese for 'the Great Ultimate' a basic principle of the universe in Chinese thought.

Tapas. Sanskrit term meaning 'austerity'. One of the means of ethical purification in Yogic meditation.

Tattva. Sanskrit term for 'category'. The term we have translated as 'category' in the expositions of, *e.g.* Jainism and of the Sankhya philosophy.

Tat Tvam Asi. Sanskrit sentence meaning 'that art thou'. The assertion identifying the Atman or inner self, with Brahman, the creator and upholder of all things, is found in the Chandogya Upanishad.

Tautology. A term that has acquired a specialized use in logic, signifying a truth-functional compound that is true for all possible assignments of truth values to its component propositions The truth-table for a tautology thus contains only Ts in the final column entered.

Te (Chinese for : power, efficacy). A term implying active moral excellence.

Techne. A Greek term referring to the knowledge and application of principles involved in the production of objects and the accomplishment of specified ends.

Teleological Argument. From 'teleology' one of the three basic arguments for God, taking the purpose, order, or design of the universe as premise for the conclusion that God exists.

Teleological Ethics. That family of ethical theories which analyze the right in terms of the ends of action. The emphasis is thus on the consequence likely to flow from decision.

Teleology

1. A doctrine that everything in the world has been designed by God to be of service to man.

2. The theory or study of purposiveness in nature: characteristically, certain phenomena seem to be best explained not by means of prior causes, but by ends or aims, intentions or purposes. Teleological explanation seems typical of living or organic things—plants, animals, people. Thus an animal's behaviour is sometimes best described in terms of its goal (food seeking, for example) a chess player's activity can be understood in terms of his purpose—to win.

Kant, in his Kritik der Urteilskraft (Critique of Judgment), wrote extensively on teleological judgments. The subject has been much discussed recently in the philosophy of science, especially in connection with biology and psychology and there have been many attempts to show how telelogical explanations do not, as they appear to, explain present events by future ones.

Telepathy. Extrasensory perception; precognition.

Temperance. One of the four Greek cardinal virtues. In Plato the specific virtue of the artisans.

Term. (in Aristotelian logic) According to Aristotle, who introduced the device of symbolizing arguments in order to exhibit their forms, a term is that 'into which the proposition is resolved, that is both the predicate and that of which it is predicated, 'being' or 'not being' being added'.

Terminist Logic. A 13th-century movement of logic in which the nature of language was strongly emphasized. The word was treated first as a physical entity, and only secondly as a significant term.

Theism. Belief in God, where God is understood to be the single omnipotent and omniscient creator of everything else that exists. He is regarded as a Being distinct from his creation though manifesting himself through it, and also essentially personal, caring for and communicating with mankind, and infinitely worthy of human worship and obedience. Theism thus is clearly a central element in the whole Judaeo-Christian religious tradition.

Theodicy. From theos ('God') and dike ('justice'). A term introduced by Leibniz to characterize the topic of God's government of the world in relation to the nature of man. The problem is the justification of God's goodness and justice in view of the evil in the world.

Theology. Theologia was originally viewed as concerned with myth. It was Aristotle who first regarded theology as a discipline, identifying it with first philosophy, the highest of the theoretical sciences, a study which was later termed metaphysics.

Theorem

(1) (of an axiomatic theory) A statement that can be proved from the axioms; that is, one that occurs as the conclusion of a valid deduction in which only axioms of the theory appear as premises.

(2) (of a natural deduction system) A statement that can be proved; that is, that occurs as the conclusion of an argument constructed according to the rules of the system and for which there are no premises.

Theory-laden. Denoting a concept, term, or statement that refers to, and can only be understood in the light of, a particular theory. For example, the phrase 'collective unconscious' makes sense only in the context of Jungian psychology.

Theosophy. An esoteric trend in religious thought. Initiates strive towards mystical insight into God's nature.

Thinking. The mental activity of (a) theoretical contemplation directed towards some object with a view to reaching a propositional conclusion; or (b) practical deliberation directed towards some object with a view to reaching a decision to act.

Thomism. The philosophy emerging from the thought of Thomas Aquinas along with the development of this thought by his followers in later centuries.

Thought. The term applies both to the process of mental activity and to its product. The interpretation of either depends upon the position one holds with respect to metaphysics, universals, and epistemology.

T'ien. Chinese term meaning 'heaven', 'the sky', 'God', 'justice'.

Time. From the Latin tempus (derived from the Greek temno, 'to cut off'). The Greek terms for 'time' are chronos and aion.

An early view identified time with cyclical movement. Various ingenious calculations were made of the extent of the world year in terms of which the cycle of existence would come to an end and begin to repeat itself. In Hinduism such cycles were related to God in his unmanifest and manifest states. For Shao Yung time moved through a repeating cycle of 129,800 years.

Plato defined time as the moving image of eternity. Time appears through the agency of the demi-urge, embodying forms in the receptacle of space.

Aristotle defined time as the numbering of motion with respect to before and after. On the ground that every 'now' implies a 'before', he concluded that time had no beginning.

Time-lag Argument. An argument casting doubt on the reliability of our perception of real physical objects. It was formulated most succinctly by Russell in Human Knowledge (p. 204).

Timocracy. From the Greek time ('honor') and kratos ('rule'). Government based on the criterion of honor. One of Plato's five types of government.

Token. Any particular specimen of any general class. All these specimens may be described as the several tokens of that single type.

Token-reflexive. Denoting a word or expression of which it is necessary to know first who is speaking or writing it, and when or where, in order to know to what particulars reference is being made.

Topic-neutral. A term describing concepts that are neutral for any particular subject matter.

Totemism. From the Ojibwa term ototeman ('brother-sister kinship'). A world-view characteristic of primitive societies in which the group regards itself as having blood relationship to a given animal (or plant).

Traducianism. The doctrine, initiated by Tertullian, that souls are passed along in the process of human generation, souls being produced from souls as bodies are produced from bodies.

Tragedy. In the Poetics, Aristotle held tragedy to be an imitation of an action by men better than or like us; the action being serious (passing from happiness to misery by necessity, or at least by probability), complete (*i,e.*, its plot having beginning, middle, and end, and in its best form containing a peripety—or reversal of the situation—and recognition), of a certain magnitude (*i.e.*, usually occurring within the limits of a single day).

Transcendent. Beyond experience. The word is often used by theists to describe the way in which God supposedly exists beyond and independent of the created world.

Transcendental Argument. An argument that answers the question : of a proposition known to be true, what conditions must be fulfilled for transcendental knowledge to be possible ?

Transcendentalism

(1) Kant's philosophy of the transcendental, and hence any theory asserting the dependence of the world of experience on the activities of reason.

(2) A mode of thought that emphasizes the intuitive and supersensuous.

(3) A form of religious mysticism.

(4) The particular doctrine adopted by a movement in New England under the leadership of Emerson and his associates, influenced by Platonism and German idealism and reacting against dogmatic rationalism.

Transcendentals. A term used by medieval philosophers to signify predicates that transcend the Aristotelian categories..

Transformation Rules. The instructions governing the transformation of one wff in a formal language into another.

Transitivity. A logical and mathematical property of transferability such that the relation x has to y and y to z, x must likewise have to z.

Trimurti. A Sanskrit term meaning 'having three shapes.' The Hindu trinity consisting of Brahma, Vishnu, and Shiva.

Truth. The putative object of knowledge and goal of inquiry, the term stands in contrast sometimes to 'falsity' and at other times to 'opinion.'

The basic theories of truth include the correspondence theory (the true 'corresponds' to reality), the coherence theory (the true is the coherent system of ideas), the pragmatic theory (the true is the 'workable' or satisfactory solution of a problematic situation), the semantic theory (assertions about truth are in a metalanguge and apply to statements of the base language), the performative theory (the assertion of truth is the performative act of agreeing with a given statement)

Criteria of truth are the marks by which we know the truth. 'Coherence' and 'workability' are examples of such criteria.

Truth Definition. A formal characterization of the set of true sentences of a language which is already used meaningfully—a characterization which is derived from an interpretation of the language. Any interpretation affords a way of describing the set of true sentences of a language.

Truth-functional (of a connective) Describing a connective when the true-value of any statement formed using it is determined in a systematic way by the truth-values of the connected statements.

Truth is Always in the Middle. A demonstrably false maxim, yet perennially appealing to those who like to see themselves as balanced and moderate judges.

Truth-table. A device, sometimes also known as a matrix, for exhibiting the conditions under which a truth-functional compound is true or false.

Truth Theory. Any account of how, given truth conditions for the semantic elements of a lauguage, the truth-values of the sentences of the language are to be determined.

Truth-value. A techical term introduced by Frege, who saw a strong analogy between concepts or predicates and mathematical functions. Consequently he thought of sentences (expressions in which a predicate is applied to an object) as standing for, or denoting, a value in the same way that 3^2 denotes 9, the value of the function x^2 for $x=3$. When a statement is, or is evaluated as true, it is said to have the truth-value True (indicated by T) and when it is fale it is said to have the ruth-value False (indicated by F).

Type. The term seems to have been derived from something like the contrast between a seal and its imprint.

For Plato and Aristo le the term was applied to schematic representations or summary images.

In logic the relation between token and type is roughly that of the meaning of a word to its written or spoken instance.

Types, Theory of. Russell's attempt to deal with the problem of self-reference. He produced two versions of the theory—the simple and the ramified. The problem itself is famously illustrated by the assertion of Epimenides the Cretan 'All Cretans are always liars'.

Tyranny. A form of governments based on absolute rule, the decisions of the ruler serving as law and constitution.

U

Uncertainty Principle. A law of physics, first stated in 1927 by Werner Heisenberg (1901-76), that has profoundly affected quantum theory and the theory of causation. It states that the position and momentum of a particle cannot both be known without uncertainty because the process of establishing either must affect the other. If Δp is the uncertainty in position and Δq that of momentum, then $\Delta p \Delta q = h/4\pi$, where h is the Planck Constant.

Unconscious, The. The doctrine that a portion of man's mental processes or memories exists below the threshold of consciousness.

Undistributed Middle, Fallacy of the. An argument in which the proposed conclusion is invalidly attained because one of the premises needs to be and is not a distributed assertion.

Uniformity of Nature, Principle of the. The principle of induction that similar occurrences follow from similar conditions.

Unitarianism. The religious doctrine that God is one, and that Jesus is to be regarded as human and not as a supernatural being.

Unit Class. A class having a single member.

Unity. From the Latin unitas ('one'). Thus the character of being one thing, event, idea, society, or whatever.

Universalism. The doctrine that all men will be saved.

Universalizability. The principle that, while individual moral judgments may be particular, they will always imply a universal judgment.

Universals and Particulars. Things are particulars and their qualities are universals. So a universal is a property predicated of all the individuals of a certain sort or class. Redness is a universal, predicated of all red objects. Universals have been claimed by some philosophers to have an existence distinct from the particular things instantiating the property. For Plato and Platonists, the observed world is only a reflection of the real world, consisting for Plato of the Forms, which are something like universals.

Universe. 'Universe' is defined as including everything there is, with the exception of the creator God, if such there be.

Universe of Discourse. A system of concepts and entities related to a particular topic or area of interest, within which certain terms and expressions acquire their own meaning or significance.

Univocal. Having only one meaning. Compare equivocal; equivocate.

Upanishads, the. The basic philosophical texts of Hinduism.

Uppsala School of Philosophy. Hagerstrom.

Utilitarian Calculus. The principle in Utilitarian ethics by which the right act is determined. It is a calculation of the greatest pleasure or least pain to all concerned.

Utilitarianism. The doctrine that the principle of greatest utility should be the criterion in ethical matters, and that the criterion is to be applied to the consequences flowing from ethical decisions. The principle is often expressed as the greatest happiness, or the greatest good, for the greatest number.

Utility. From the Latin utilis ('useful'). In the philosophic tradition a property of those things which have value not io theselves but as a means to some end.

Utility, Principle of. The greatest happiness principle.

Utopia. From the Greek ou ('not') plus topos ('a place'). It has been used by philosophers, social thinkers, and novelists to refer to any ideal, unrealizable social structure. In what follows we shall classify utopias according to the division suggested above, while recognizing the inevitability of overlap among the classes.

Uttara Mimamsa. The system of Indian philosoyhy usually known as Vedanta.

Utopianism. The beliefs of those concerned to establish not just a better but a perfect society.

Uttara Mimamsa. A Sanskrit term literally meaning 'the later revered thought' and referring to a school of Indian thought dealing with the latter portion of the Vedas. The school is better known as Vedanta, meaning 'end of the Vedas'.

V

Vacuous. In logic, describing the status of sentences that are true because their subject terms have no denotation or because their antecedents are false.

Vagueness. A word or term is said to be vague, or to have the property, 'vaguenss,' when there are borderline cases and uncertainty concerning whether or not the term applies to these cases.

Vaibhasika. One of the four chief philosophical schools of Buddhism, standing for the epistemology of direct realism, and belonging to Hinayana Buddhism.

Vaiseshika. A Sanskrit term meaning 'particularity.' Vaiseshika is one of the six systems of Indian thought to arise in the period following the Vedic age. The Vaiseshika Sutra was composed by Kanada, sometime after 300 B.C. The system and sutra contain the following ideas :

(1) Sensible things are composed of invisible atoms, eternal in nature, and bearing one of four characteristics : earth, water, light, and air.

(2) Also eternal are the souls which pervade certain bodies for a time. Each individual soul has its individual characteristic, and this is true even after the soul has been freed from the body.

(3) In sum, there are nine substances : earth, water, light, air, ether time, space, soul, and mind.

(4) In the Vaiseshika Sutra God is not mentioned; but commentators borrowed the Nyaya conception of God to complete the system.

(5) The categories of experience are : substance, quality, activity, generality, particularity, inherence, and non-existence.

Vaishnavism. Hindu sect.

Vaisyas. The commercial class of Indian tradition.

Valid and Invalid. Terms that may be applied to arguments or to patterns or forms of argument. An argument is valid when it is impossible for its premises to be true and its conclusion false; it is invalid otherwise.

Validity. A concept of logic characteristic of sound arguments. Validity must be carefully distinguished from truth.

Validity and Truth. Validity in symbolic logic, a term applicable to arguments, is defined by reference to the possible truth-values of the component sentences of arguments. If the argument 'P_1.. P_n, therefore C' is valid, it must be impossible for C to be false when P_1...P_n are all true. This will be the case iff the material conditional statement 'P_1&...& $\supset$ C is always true. If P_1 . P_n, C are all truth, functional compounds, to say that 'P_1&.. &P_n $\supset$ C' is always true is to say that it is a tautology.

Value. A theory of value is a theory about what things in the world are good, desirable, and important.

Value, Final. That value, or set of values, at which all men do or should aim.

Value-freedom. The ideal, recommended by Max Weber, that social scientists should eschew value-judgments about people and institutions within their fields of study.

Value Theory. The designation, along with Axiology, for the field of philosophy investigating the nature of value and valuataion.

Vardhamana (Mahavira). 599-527 B.C. Indian philosopher and religious leader. A leader of the Jains, Vardhamana systematized the doctrines of the movement in terms of his understanding of the traditional founders, Rsabha, Ajitanatha, and Aristanemi. All three of these men are mentioned in the Yajur Veda, a document central to Jainism.

Variable. Originally a symbol introduced as a place-holder for an expression of some specified kind.

Variables have come to be used extensively in logic. For example, propositional variables, usually 'p', 'q', 'r', are used in representing the possible forms of complex propositions, such as 'p → (q V r)'. Individual variables, usually 'x', 'y', 'z', are used to indicate places for names of objects in expressions for functions, whether propositional or mathematical, as in 'x is the brother of y'. These are examples of free occurrences of variables, that is, occurrences of variables where they can be replaced by particular expressions of the appropriate kind.

Varuna. Once chief among the Vedic divinities, Varuna was the sky god guaranteeing cosmic order.

Vasubandhu. 4th or 5th cent. A.D. Indian philosopher. Brother of Asanga founder of the Way of Yoga, Vasubandhu was known as the systematizer of the school.

Principal writings : The Treatise in Twenty Stanzas on Representation-only (T); The Thirty Verses on the Mind-only Doctrine (T).

Vedanta. From the Sanskrit veda ('knowledge') and anta ('end'). One of the six philosophical systems of India, arising after the period of the Vedas, and in response to the heterodox systems. The chief interpretations of Vedanta are three :

(1) The most widely admired and accepted view, Advaita Vedanta, is that of Shankara in this non-dual interpretation Brahman is the sole reality, the world is an appearance and Brahman and Atman are identical.

(2) The interpretation of Ramanuja admits the reality of God, selves, and world, although the two latter exist only as the body of God, who has two forms.

(3) The interpretation of Madhva allows the permanent individuality of God, selves, and matter, and provides an organic interpretation of the nature of existing things.

The Vedas. Sanskrit term meaning 'knowledge'. The Vedas are an ancient Indian collection of hymns, rituals, regulations for religious sacrifices, and philosophical essays. The Vedas divide into the following divisions.

(1) There are the Samhitas. These are hymns addressed to gods and goddesses, and were used in the Vedic sacrifices. There are four collections of Samhitas : the Rig Sama, Yajur, and Atharva—one for each of the four main priests of the sacrifice.

(2) The Brahmanas deal with the rules for the sacrifices.

(3) Added on to the Brahmanas are the Aranyakas. These interpret the meaning of the Vedic sacrifices. Composed in forest retreats the Aranyakas venture from mysticism into philosophic thought.

(4) The Upanishads form the concluding portions of the Aranyakas, and represent the height of Vedic philosophy. The Upanishads are also known as the Vedanta, which means 'the end of the Veda'.

(5) The sutras form a late stage of Vedic literature, expressing in aphoristic form the essential requirements of the Vedic religion. The sutras deal with priestly matters, domestic rites. social duties, philosophy, magic, astronomy, etc. The Dharma Sutras deal with the questions of one's social duties. The Laws of Manu is the chief of the Dharma Sutras, and of ancient Hindu codes.

Veil of Appearance. Sense data viewed, as interposing between the experiencer and the external world.

Venn Diagrams. A more powerful way of representing class relationships than the Euler diagrams (Euler), this type of diagrammatic representation allows one to check the validity of syllogistic inferences by means of three overlapping circles, standing for the terms of the syllogism. The method was developed by John Venn.

Veridical. Telling the truth.

Verifiability. The condition of admitting verification. Verification is any procedure carried out to determine whether a statement is true or false. A statement which might be shown to be true is said to be in principle verifiable.

Verification (or verifiability) Principle. The criterion of meaningfulness applied by the logical positivists to any proposition.

Vicious Circle Principle. An explanation of certain logical paradoxes discussed in Russel's theory of types. A vicious circle is generated whenever it is supposed that 'a collection of objects may contain members which can only be defined by means of the collection as a whole'.

Vienna Circle of Logical Positivists. A reform movement in philosophy centering in the University of Vienna in the 1920's and '30's. The movement was directed toward the achievement of a scientific philosophy, and the elimination of pseudopropositions, including the propositions of metaphysics.

Vijnanavada. A school of Mahayana 'Buddhist philosophy. Intense contemplation on an object had shown that it was possible to conjure up a mental image of it which appeared as 'real' as the original, and combining this insight with the teaching about the 'emptiness' of all phenomena the Vijnanavada postulated that both the objects of the external world and the perceiving subjects are merely the illusory projections of universal Consciousness (vijnana, also tathata : 'thusness').

Vindication. A justification of induction that seeks to show that, although it may be quite indeterminate as to whether induction will work or not, it is rational to use it because it will work if any method will. The future Universe may be regular or chaotic. It it is regular, induction will be the best policy. If chaotic, no method will be applicable so the user of induction will be no worse off than anyone else.

Virtue. Although the initial sense of the term included the meanings of "strength," "couraye," and "excellence," an ethical signification quickly arose, and has remained central. In recent discussion "virtue", and "vice" have been largely replaced: in the singular by "good" and" evil," "right" and "wrong;" and in the plural by "values" and "disvalues."

Vishnu. Hindu God. Center of worship in the great Vaisnava or Vishnuite sect of Hinduism. In the Hindu trimurti, or trinity, Vishnu is the preserver where Brahma creates and Shiva destroys.

Vishnuism. Hindu sect.

Vitalism. The name given to that interpretation of biological phenomena which assumes the presence of some force or principle within the organism not reducible to the categories of physics and chemistry. In the case of Hans Driesch the vital force is said to be a directing and supporting entelechy.

Void. In Pythagorean cosmogony, the factor in the Universe by means of which units could be separated and distinguished.

Volition. An act of will preceding a physical movement. What is the difference between my arm going up and my raising my arm? The traditional answer is that in the second case the physical movement was preceded by a prior volitional act.

Voluntarism.

1. A certain sort of metaphysics (of which Schopenhauer's is typical), that holds that the true nature of reality is will.

2. In controversies about the nature of history, a theory that attaches too much weight to the human will as a factor in history, and too little to 'objective', that is economic, factors. Marxists often accuse other Marxists of 'voluntarism' of this kind.

Voting Paradox. A paradox that illustrates a fatal flaw in the attempt to determine the "collective preference" of a community by means of a simple majority voting system.

W

Weakness of The Will. The state of mind an agent in said to be in when he performs an intentional action that goes against his better judgment.

Weber-fechner Law. A psychophysical law (S=C log R) according to which the intensity of sensation (S) is equal to the logarithm of its stimulus (R) given a constant (C).

Weltanschauung. (German for : world outlook). The term used for the general view of the Universe and man's relationship to it. Usually the term is applied to a philosophy affecting the practical (as opposed to purely theoretical) attitudes and beliefs of its adherents.

Wff. Acronym for "well-formed formula." A well-formed formula refers to one which conforms to the requirements of the system of which it is a part.

Will. The term refers to a potency, faculty, or force in man involved in decision-making. The view that the will is dominant over the reason is termed "voluntarism". The view that reason is determinative over will is termed "intellectualism." or simply "rationalism". In addition there are views providing a balance between reason and will.

Will to Believe. A concept of William James to the effect that we can believe beyond the evidence in cases where our options are forced, living, and momentous.

Wisdom. Plato viewed wisdom as one of the four chief, or cardinal, virtues. It concerned 'knowledge of the whole'. The path to wisdom required both scientific knowledge and practical experience.

Word, The. Unamuno regarded the World as the intimate expression of the man of flesh and bone; while Heidegger found the Word present in all discourse and capable of revelatory disclosures of Being.

World Soul. Refers to an analogue, in the world as a whole, of the human soul or mind. Anti-materialist (compare materialism) in conception, the idea is founded on the view that the world is productive of life and animation, and can therefore be regarded as itself animate.

Wu Wei. A Chinese term meaning 'inaction' or 'taking no unnatural action'. A central term in the history of Taoism, the concept is stressed in the Tao-Te-Ching. It is found in Taoist leaders such as Chuang Tzu and Huai-nan Tzu.

X

Xenophanes. 570-c. 470 B.C. Greek philosopher. Born in Colophon. Exiled from his home, probably by a Persian victory.

Holding that there is no certain knowledge about the gods or any other matter, Xenophanes pointed out that men create gods in their own image, just as animals would make them like themselves had they the ability to draw.

Xenophon, c. 430-c. 355 B.C. Greek writer and moralist. Born in Athens. An active participant in civic life, Xenophon was one of the young Athenians who felt friendship for Socrates. After the latter's death, Xenophon, although not himself a philosopher, answered the charges that Socrates was guilty of impiety and corrupting the youth. The charges had been made at the trial and were repeated later by Polycrates. Xenophon replied to the charges in his his Memorabilia by picturing Socrates as a teacher of virtue and practical knowledge who exerted a beneficial influence on all who knew him.

Y

Yahweh. The name of the God of Israel, originally written 'YHWH, without the vowels, as a sign of reverence.

Yajur Veda. One of the four Vedas of early Hinduism, the Yajur Veda is highly ritualistic in character.

Yasna. One of the five parts of the Avesta, sacred scriptures of Zoroastrianism.

Yin Yang Philosophy. A Chinese doctrine, not the product of a school of philosophy or of a particular distinguished philosopher, but a natural development which has influenced most Chinese philosophers, and many aspects of Chinese life. This following ideas are relevant :

1. Reality is in constant change, and this change is to be explained by the interaction of two primal elements, forces, or principles : yin, the female principle, negative, passive,

weak, yielding : and yang, the male principle, positive, active, strong, assertive. The respective force of these principles in objects and events determines their character.

2. The five elements—metal, wood, water, fire, earth—provide a matrix for the working of yin and yang.

3. The notion of fives was elaborated into other areas. There are the five activities : appearance, speech, seeing, hearing, thinking. This five parts of time : year, month, day, zodiacal distinctions, and the calendric calculations. The five blessings : longevity, wealth, health, virtue, and an end crowings life. In addition there are the five directions, the five musical notes, five sense organs, five metals, five virtues, five feelings, and five social relations.

Yoga. A Sanskrit term meaning both 'yoke' and 'union'. Thus, a practical means of discipline leading to union of the individual self and the universal soul. The term may also derive from the root yuj ('to contemplate').

Yogachara. Sanskrit term meaning 'the way of Yoga.'

opponents of Parmenides of Elea, in particular the Pythagoreans. First, there were about 40 putative refutations of plurality, of which only two survive. Second, there were the four perennially, fascinating arguments against motion. Either space and time are infinitely divisible, in which case motion is continuous and smooth-flowing, or else there are indivisible minima, in which case motion is fundamentally cinematographic, proceeding ultimately in tiny jerks.

Zetetic. From the Greek zetesis ('art of inquiry'). Hence, one who engages in inquiry or the act itself.

Zionism. From the Hebrew tsiyon ("Jerusalem'). The name given to the movement for the return of Jews to the promised land for the purpose of establishing a national state in Palestine.

Zoroaster. The name is a corrupt Greek form of the Iranian 'Zarathustra.' His date is a matter for conjecture, but he probably lived some time after 1000 B.C. He was founder of the Zoroastrain religion, which endured until crushed by the persecutions following the Mohammedan invarsion of 636 A.D.

Z

Za-zen. The term for meditation in Zen Buddhism.

Zen Buddhism. Called Zen in Japan, Ch'an in China (both terms signifying 'meditation'), a form of religion which developed out of, and in reaction to, Hinayana and Mahayana Buddhism.

Zeno's Paradoxes. The genius of Zeno of Elea was displayed in developing two sets of arguments designed to discredit